The Big Book of
Strip Quilts

Start with Strips to Make
60 Stunning Quilts

Martingale
Create with Confidence

The Big Book of Strip Quilts:
Start with Strips to Make 60 Stunning Quilts
© 2017 by Martingale & Company®

Martingale®
19021 120th Ave. NE, Ste. 102
Bothell, WA 98011-9511 USA
ShopMartingale.com

Printed in China
22 21 20 19 18 17   8 7 6 5 4 3 2 1

Library of Congress Cataloging-in-Publication Data

Title: The big book of strip quilts.

Description: Bothell, WA : Martingale, 2017.

Identifiers: LCCN 2016047939 (print) | LCCN 2016048621 (ebook)
   | ISBN 9781604688542 | ISBN 9781604688740 ()

Subjects: LCSH: Strip quilting--Patterns. | Patchwork--Patterns.

Classification: LCC TT835 .B4887 2017 (print) | LCC TT835 (ebook)
   | DDC 746.46--dc23

LC record available at https://lccn.loc.gov/2016047939

MISSION STATEMENT

We empower makers who use fabric and yarn to make life more enjoyable.

CREDITS

PUBLISHER AND
CHIEF VISIONARY OFFICER
Jennifer Erbe Keltner

CONTENT DIRECTOR
Karen Costello Soltys

DESIGN MANAGER
Adrienne Smitke

MANAGING EDITOR
Tina Cook

COVER AND TEXT DESIGNER
Regina Girard

ACQUISITIONS EDITOR
Karen M. Burns

PHOTOGRAPHER
Brent Kane

COPY EDITOR
Melissa Bryan

Contents

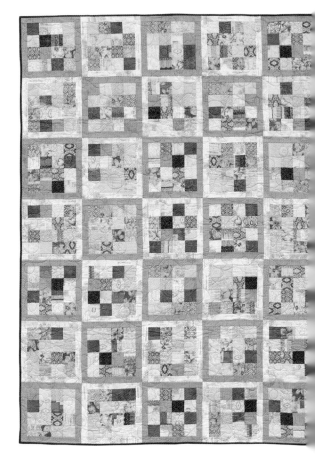

Introduction

////////////

They call to us from quilt-shop shelves, neatly rolled in bundles or cleverly staggered in packages where we can see the slightest bit of their fabric splendor. They are many a quilter's favorite precut, just enough to satisfy the desire to own a little piece (2½" × 42" to be exact) of every piece in a fabric collection. Sometimes we cut them ourselves with fabric left over from our latest project. Or perhaps we've swapped them with friends. But regardless of how we've come to acquire them, the truth is we're almost powerless to resist them. After all, what quilter doesn't relish the small but mighty 2½" strip?

Well, fellow strip lovers, your dreams of making something with all those fabric strips you've stockpiled, stashed, and stored are about to come true. You hold in your hands dozens of quilt solutions! With 60 patterns to choose from, there truly is something for everyone in these pages. And best of all, every quilt in this book starts with that same magical fabric precut—the 2½" strip.

In some cases the strips used in a quilt are all from a single collection. In other cases they're a scrappy assortment from the designer's stash. All of the designers will dazzle you with their ability to turn a simple strip into a dynamic quilt. Enjoy the array. Our guess is, much the same way you acquired that collection of fabric strips you own, you're going to have a tough time choosing just one!

Blueberry Pie

How does a sweet dessert lead to a sweet quilt? When a designer like Kathy Brown takes inspiration from memories of her mom's blueberry pie, transforming them into a yummy blueberry-and-crust quilted homage.

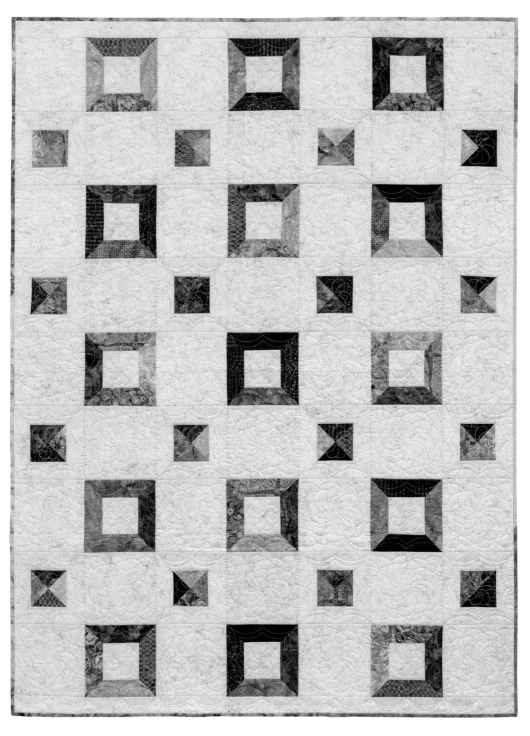

FINISHED QUILT: 56½" × 72½" • **FINISHED BLOCK:** 8" × 8"

Designed by Kathy Brown; pieced by Linda Reed; quilted by Carol Hilton

Materials

Yardage is based on 42"-wide fabric.

15 precut strips, 2½" × 42", of assorted blue tone on tones for blocks and binding

15 precut strips, 2½" × 42", of assorted brown tone on tones for blocks and binding

4⅛ yards of cream tone on tone for blocks and border

4 yards of fabric for backing

64" × 80" piece of batting

Cutting

From the cream tone on tone, cut:

26 strips, 2½" × 42"

8 strips, 8½" × 42"; crosscut into 32 squares, 8½" × 8½"

Making the Blocks

Press the seam allowances as indicated by the arrows, or as otherwise instructed.

1 With right sides together, sew a cream strip to a blue strip. Repeat to make a total of 11 blue strip sets. Sew a cream strip to a brown strip. Repeat to make a total of 11 brown strip sets. Set aside the remaining blue and brown strips for the binding.

Make 11.

Make 11.

2 Referring to "Cutting Triangles" on page 9, cut six 90° double-strip triangles from each strip set.

3 Separate the triangles into four sets of 33 triangles each. (Note: You'll have one each of the cream tip/blue strip, blue tip/cream strip, and brown tip/cream strip triangles left over, and five of the cream tip/brown strip triangles left over.)

- cream tip/blue strip
- blue tip/cream strip
- cream tip/brown strip
- brown tip/cream strip

Make 33 of each.

4 With right sides together, join four assorted cream tip/blue strip triangles as shown. Repeat to make a total of eight Blueberry Pie blocks.

Blueberry Pie block.
Make 8.

5 Repeat step 4 to make seven Crust blocks using four assorted cream tip/brown strip triangles and 16 Ice Cream-and-Pie blocks using two assorted blue tip/cream strip triangles and two assorted brown tip/cream strip triangles.

Crust block.   Ice Cream-and-Pie block.
Make 7.   Make 16.

Assembling the Quilt Top

1. Lay out the blocks and cream 8½" squares in nine rows as shown in the quilt assembly diagram below.

2. Sew the pieces together into rows and press the seam allowances in opposite directions from row to row. Sew the rows together and press the seam allowances in one direction.

3. Join two cream 2½" × 42" strips end to end. Repeat to make a second pieced strip. Sew the strips to the top and bottom of the quilt top for the border; press and trim.

Finishing the Quilt

Go to ShopMartingale.com/HowtoQuilt if you need more information on finishing techniques.

1. Layer and baste your quilt, and quilt as desired.

2. Using the remaining blue and brown 2½"-wide strips, prepare and attach the binding.

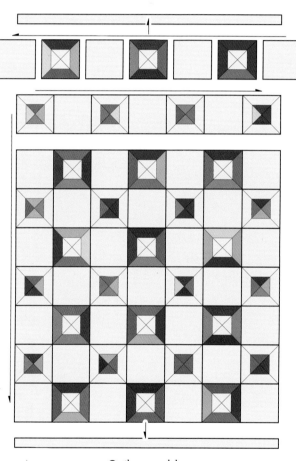

Quilt assembly

When cutting triangles, designer Kathy Brown recommends using the 90° Double-Strip ruler from Creative Grids. It's simple, fast, and accurate. To help ensure success, Kathy also advises starching and pressing your strip sets before proceeding. The cuts you make with this ruler produce bias edges, and starch helps prevent these edges from stretching. Press straight and do not stretch the sets by twisting or turning the iron. A simple up-and-down, side-to-side motion will ensure straight sets.

Follow the guidelines below for left-hand or right-hand cutting; ruler placement remains the same.

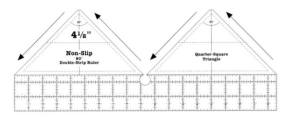

Right-hand cutting: follow the ruler from right to left.

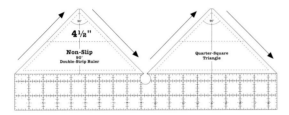

Left-hand cutting: follow the ruler from left to right.

1. Lay the strip ruler down on top of a strip set (strip set right side up), lining up the left edge of the ruler approximately 1" to the right of the beginning of the strip set, the bottom edge of the triangles on the ruler with the bottom edge of the strip set, and the middle dashed line on the ruler with the middle seamline of the strip set.

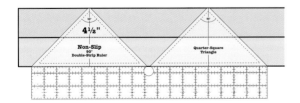

2. Cut the first set of triangles—three in all. The remainder of the strip set will look something like that shown below. Proceed to the next step.

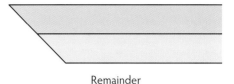

Remainder

3. Rotate the remainder of the strip set 180° so the fabric strip that was along the top is now along the bottom. Once again, lay your strip ruler down on top of the strip set, this time lining up the *right* sloping edge of the ruler with the cut angle of the strip set, the bottom edge of the triangles on the ruler with the bottom edge of the strip set, and the middle dashed seamline on the ruler with the middle seamline of the strip set. Cut a second set of triangles.

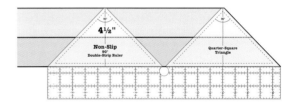

Illustrated below are the triangle shapes that result from one strip set made from precut 2½" × 42" strips.

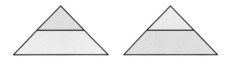

The 90° Double-Strip ruler is not the only tool that will work for this technique. You can use any right-angle triangle ruler that has marked lines parallel to the base of the triangle that measure 2¼" and 4½" from the tip of the triangle. Align the 4½" line on the triangle ruler with the bottom of the strip set, and the 2¼" line with the strip-set seam line. Cut along both sloping edges of the triangle ruler. To cut each subsequent triangle, rotate the strip set 180°, line up the right sloping edge of the ruler with the cut angle of the strip set, and cut another triangle.

Cabin in the Clouds

Cut fluffy clouds from Cuddle fabric, which is incredibly soft and easy to sew. The thick pile of the Cuddle fabric hides stitches, freeing you from turning the edges and allowing you to make quick work of the hand-stitched appliqué.

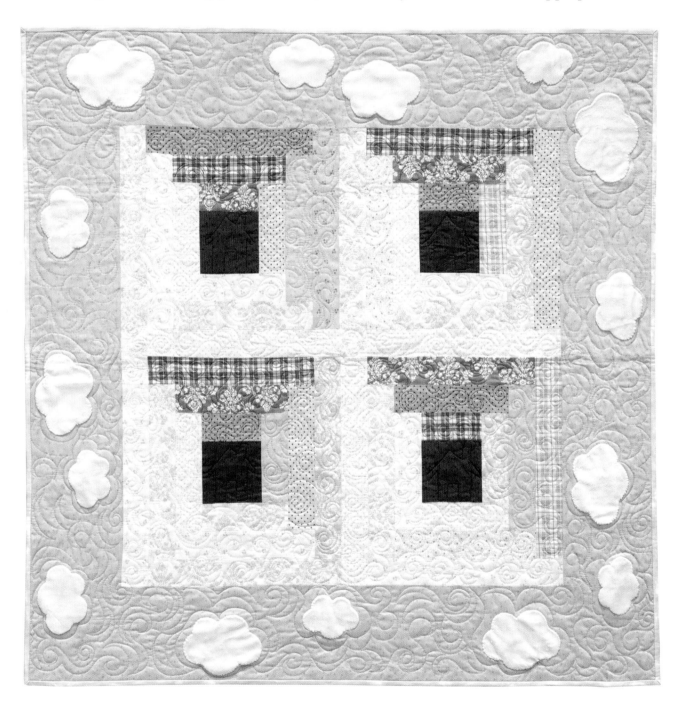

FINISHED QUILT: 46" × 46" • **FINISHED BLOCK:** 16" × 16"

Designed, pieced, hand appliquéd, and quilted by Cassie Barden

Materials

Yardage is based on 42"-wide fabric, unless otherwise specified.

7 precut strips, 2½" × 42", of at least 4 different tan prints for blocks

4 precut strips, 2½" × 42", of at least 3 different medium blue prints for blocks

4 precut strips, 2½" × 42", of at least 3 different medium brown prints for blocks

¼ yard of dark brown print for block centers

1¼ yards of blue print A for border

⅓ yard of 58"-wide cream Cuddle or Minky fabric for clouds

½ yard of blue print B for binding

2 yards of fabric for backing

52" × 52" piece of batting

Appliqué needle and thread

Cutting

Lay out your blocks as you cut the strips to get a combination that looks nice and scrappy. Mix the fabrics within a color group so there are different prints cut the same size. Patterns for the clouds are on pages 14 and 15.

From the dark brown print, cut:
4 squares, 4½" × 4½"

From the 4 brown print strips, cut a *total* of:
4 strips, 2½" × 4½"
4 strips, 2½" × 8½"
4 strips, 2½" × 12½"

From the 4 blue print strips, cut a *total* of:
4 strips, 2½" × 6½"
4 strips, 2½" × 10½"
4 strips, 2½" × 14½"

From the 7 tan print strips, cut a *total* of:
4 strips, 2½" × 6½"
4 strips, 2½" × 8½"
4 strips, 2½" × 10½"
4 strips, 2½" × 12½"
4 strips, 2½" × 14½"
4 strips, 2½" × 16½"

From blue print A, cut:
2 strips, 7½" × 32½"
3 strips, 7½" × 42"

From the Cuddle or Minky fabric, cut:*
3 extra-large clouds
4 large clouds
4 medium clouds
4 small clouds

From blue print B, cut:
5 strips, 2½" × 42"

*Cuddle and Minky fabrics have a nap (the direction in which the fabric feels smooth). Cut each cloud with the nap running from the top of the cloud to the bottom.

Making the Blocks

Press the seam allowances as indicated by the arrows, or as otherwise instructed.

1 Sew a medium brown 2½" × 4½" strip to one side of a dark brown 4½" square. Repeat for all four dark brown squares and 2½" × 4½" strips.

2 Rotate a step 1 unit 90°, with the 2½" × 4½" strip on top. Sew a medium blue 2½" × 6½" strip to one long edge of the first unit as shown. Sew a tan 2½" × 6½" strip to the bottom edge of the unit as shown. Sew a tan 2½" × 8½" strip to the final edge of the unit to complete the first log cabin round. Repeat with the remaining three units from step 1.

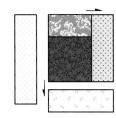 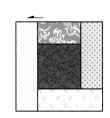

3 Sew the second round of strips in the same manner as the first, starting by sewing a medium brown 2½" × 8½" strip to the same edge as the first strip sewn. From here on, you can always tell what side to sew the strip to—it's the side with two seams. Press all seam allowances away from the center.

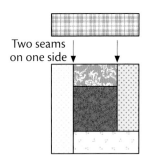
Two seams on one side

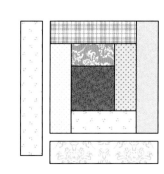

4 Sew the third round of strips in the same manner, pressing away from the center. Complete all three rounds to make four Log Cabin blocks.

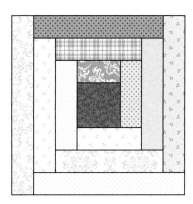
Make 4.

Assembling the Quilt Top

1 Lay out two rows of two blocks each. Position the blocks as shown or rotate them as desired.

2 Sew the blocks together into rows, and then sew the rows together.

3 Sew the blue A 7½" × 32½" strips to the sides of the quilt top. Join the blue A 7½" × 42" strips end to end. Press the seam allowances open. Cut the pieced strip into two strips, 46½" long. Sew the strips to the top and bottom of the quilt top to complete the border.

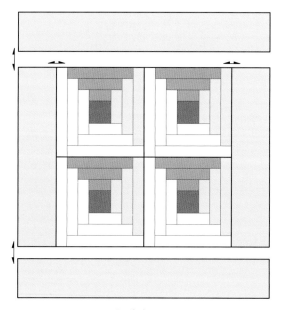
Quilt layout

4 Referring to the quilt photo on page 10 for placement, whipstitch the clouds to the border. To whipstitch, tie a knot at the end of your thread and bring the needle from the back of the quilt to the front of the border fabric just under the edge of the appliqué. Insert the needle into the background fabric close to the appliqué, and bring the tip back to the front through the background and the appliqué fabric. Repeat this motion by making another diagonal stitch. Imagine making a Z shape over the edge of the appliqué. You don't have to turn under the edge, as the Cuddle fabric does not fray.

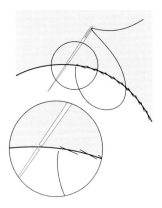

Finishing the Quilt

Go to ShopMartingale.com/HowtoQuilt if you need more information on finishing techniques.

1 Layer and baste your quilt, and quilt as desired.

2 Using the blue B 2½"-wide strips, prepare and attach the binding.

WORKING WITH PLUSH FABRICS

Plush fabrics, such as Cuddle and Minky, are wonderful to touch and perfect for baby quilts, especially as backs or appliqué. Since they are 100% polyester, however, they need to be treated differently than quilting cottons.

- Never iron Cuddle or Minky directly. At best, it will flatten the nap and the fabric won't feel as nice. At worst, it can melt the fabric! This sort of fabric doesn't wrinkle easily so it shouldn't need pressing, but if you must, you can place a towel between the iron and the fabric and press with low heat.

- Fabrics with a very short nap, like Cuddle, can be cut normally, but anything with a longer nap should be cut carefully from the back. Try to cut only the backing, and not the "fuzz," to prevent pieces from having a blunt, trimmed edge.

- These fabrics tend to shed. Shake each piece over a trash bag before sewing it onto the quilt, and keep a vacuum and lint roller handy.

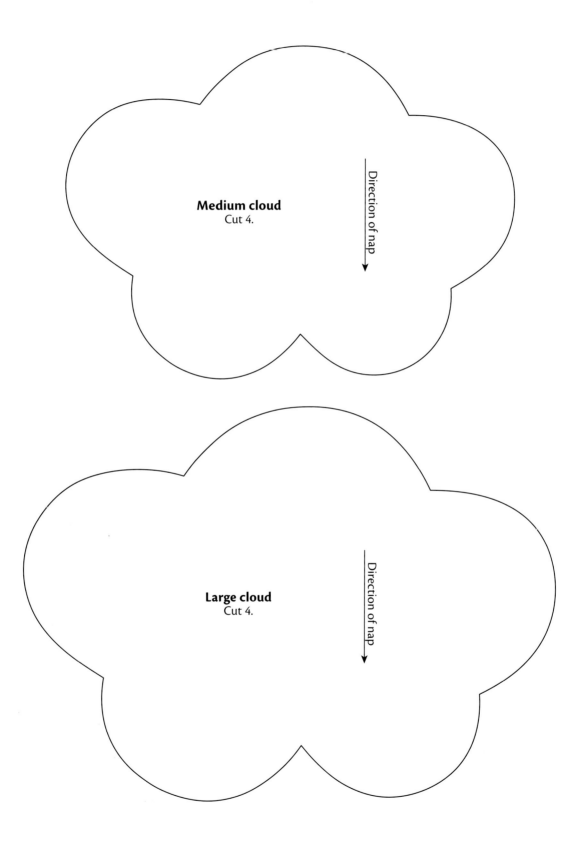

Medium cloud
Cut 4.

Direction of nap

Large cloud
Cut 4.

Direction of nap

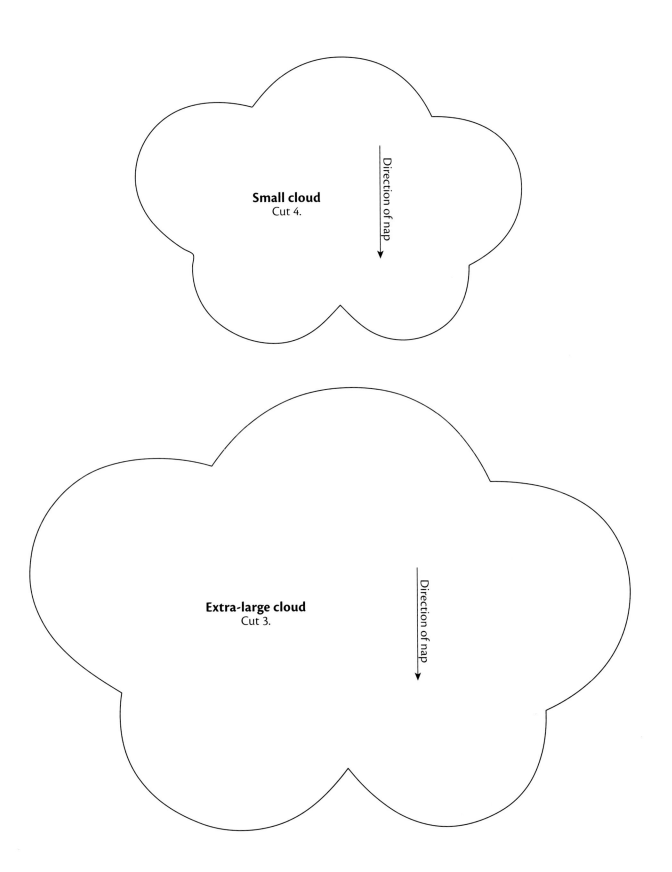

Small cloud
Cut 4.

Direction of nap

Extra-large cloud
Cut 3.

Direction of nap

Triple Star

Even though this quilt has a 1930s feel, a lot of the prints are contemporary fabrics pulled from Kim's scrap basket. Simply raid your stash, make 16 blocks using easy piecing techniques, add sashing and a border, and you're done!

FINISHED QUILT: 66½" × 66½" • **FINISHED BLOCK:** 14" × 14"

Designed, pieced, and quilted by Kim Brackett

Materials

Yardage is based on 42"-wide fabric.

32 precut strips, 2½" × 42", of assorted 1930s reproduction prints for blocks

4⅓ yards of blue solid for blocks, sashing strips, border, and binding

4½ yards of fabric for backing

73" × 73" piece of batting

Cutting

From *each* of 16 reproduction print strips, cut:

4 rectangles, 2½" × 6½" (64 total)

2 rectangles, 2½" × 4½" (32 total)

1 square, 2½" × 2½" (16 total)

From *each* of 16 reproduction print strips, cut:

4 rectangles, 2½" × 6½" (64 total)

2 rectangles, 2½" × 4½" (32 total)

From the blue solid, cut:

1 strip, 14½" × 42"; crosscut along the *lengthwise* grain into 12 strips, 2½" × 14½"

8 strips, 4½" × 42"; crosscut into 64 squares, 4½" × 4½"

35 strips, 2½" × 42"; crosscut *16 strips* into 256 squares, 2½" × 2½"

CUTTING FROM YOUR STASH

Time to whittle down your fabric stash? To cut your blocks from scraps rather than using precut 2½" strips as listed in "Materials" above, follow these instructions.

From assorted 1930s reproduction prints, cut:

128 rectangles, 2½" × 6½"

64 rectangles, 2½" × 4½"

16 squares, 2½" × 2½"

From assorted background fabrics, cut:

16 sets of:
- 4 squares, 4½" × 4½" (64 total)
- 16 squares, 2½" × 2½" (256 total)

Making the Blocks

Press the seam allowances as indicated by the arrows, or as otherwise instructed.

1 Draw a diagonal line from corner to corner on the wrong side of a blue 2½" square. Place the marked square on one end of a print 2½" × 4½" rectangle, right sides together and corners aligned. Sew on the line. Trim the excess corner fabric, leaving a ¼" seam allowance, and press. Make four units.

Make 4.

2 Sew a blue 4½" square to each unit from step 1 as shown. Make four.

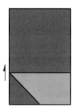

Make 4.

3 Referring to the technique used in step 1, place a marked blue 2½" square on one end of a print 2½" × 6½" rectangle. Stitch, trim, and press. Make four.

Make 4.

4 Sew a unit from step 3 to the right edge of each unit from step 2. Make four.

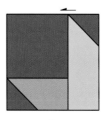

Make 4.

5 Referring to the technique used in step 1, place marked blue 2½" squares on opposite ends of a print 2½" × 6½" rectangle, paying careful attention to the directions of the sewing lines. Stitch, trim, and press. Make four.

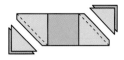

Make 4.

6 Arrange and sew together the units from step 4, the units from step 5, and one print 2½" square as shown. Make a total of 16 blocks.

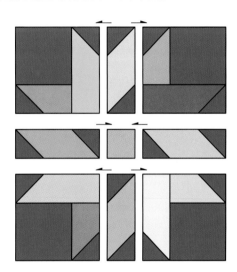

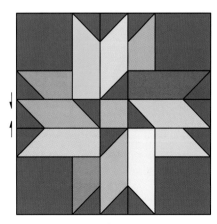

Make 16.

Assembling the Quilt Top

1 Join five blue 2½" × 42" strips end to end. From the long strip, cut three sashing strips, 62½" long.

2 Lay out the blocks and the blue 2½" × 14½" strips in four rows of four blocks and three vertical sashing strips each, with the 62½" sashing strips placed horizontally between the rows. Join the blocks and vertical strips into rows. Sew the rows and the horizontal strips together.

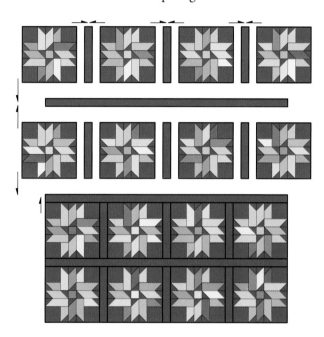

3 Join the remaining blue 2½"-wide strips end to end. Measure the length of the quilt top through the center. Cut two strips to that measurement and sew them to the sides of the quilt top. Press the seam allowances away from the center. Measure the width of the quilt top through the center, including the borders just added. Cut two strips to that measurement and sew them to the top and bottom of the quilt top to complete the border. Press the seam allowances away from the center.

Finishing the Quilt

Go to ShopMartingale.com/HowtoQuilt if you need more information on finishing techniques.

1 Layer and baste your quilt, and quilt as desired.

2 Using the remaining blue 2½"-wide strips, prepare and attach the binding.

Knotted Squares

Bold, geometric lines pair with whimsical floral prints. It's a study in contrasts that amounts to a beauty of a quilt. Enhance that beauty by taking advantage of the open spaces, filling them with dense quilting.

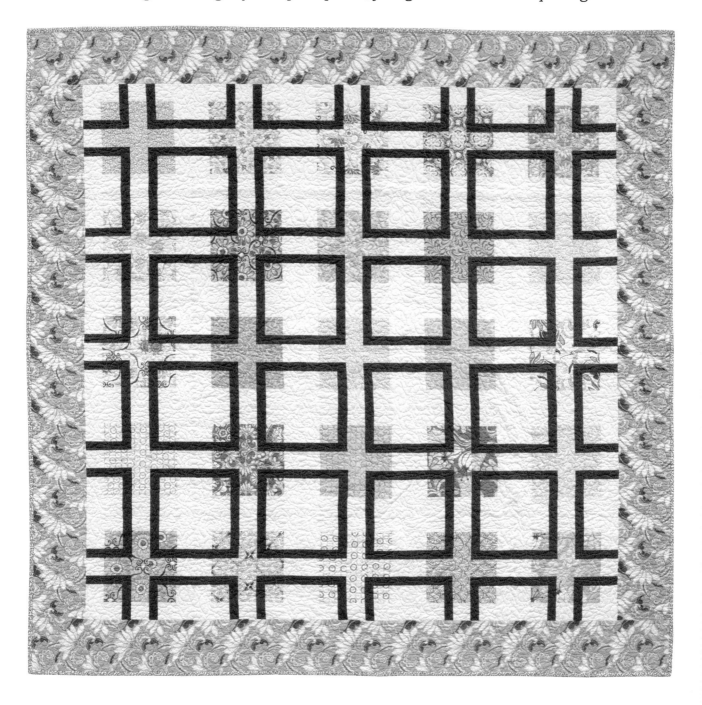

FINISHED QUILT: 72½" × 72½" • **FINISHED BLOCK:** 12" × 12"

Designed and pieced by Amy Ellis; quilted by Natalia Bonner

Materials

Yardage is based on 42"-wide fabric.

25 precut strips, 2½" × 42", of assorted prints
    for blocks
2 yards of white solid for blocks
1⅓ yards of brown solid for blocks
2¼ yards of green print for border
⅝ yard of coral print for binding
4½ yards of fabric for backing
78" × 78" piece of batting

Cutting

From *each* of the 25 print strips, cut:
1 strip, 2½" × 10½" (25 total)
2 rectangles, 2½" × 3½" (50 total)
1 rectangle, 2½" × 8½" (25 total)

From the white solid, cut:
27 strips, 2½" × 42"; crosscut into:
    25 strips, 2½" × 10½"
    100 squares, 2½" × 2½"
    100 rectangles, 2½" × 4½"

From the brown solid, cut:
28 strips, 1½" × 42"; crosscut into:
    100 rectangles, 1½" × 4½"
    100 rectangles, 1½" × 5½"

From the green print, cut on the *lengthwise* grain:
2 strips, 6½" × 60½"
2 strips, 6½" × 72½"

From the coral print, cut:
8 strips, 2½" × 42"

Making the Blocks

Press the seam allowances as indicated by the arrows,
or as otherwise instructed.

1   Pin and sew a white 2½" × 10½" strip to a print
2½" × 10½" strip along the long edges. Make 25
strip sets.

Make 25 strip sets.

2   Cut each strip set into four segments, 2½" × 4½",
for a total of 100 segments.

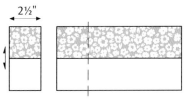

Cut 4 segments from each strip set.

3   Sew a white 2½" × 4½" rectangle to each unit from
step 2 as shown.

Make 100.

4   Sew a brown 1½" × 4½" rectangle to each unit
from step 3 as shown.

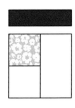

Make 100.

5   Sew a brown 1½" × 5½" rectangle to each unit
from step 4 as shown. Trim to 5½" square if
necessary. Make 100 units.

Make 100.

6   Sew a white 2½" square to one end of a print
2½" × 3½" rectangle as shown. Make 50 units.

Make 50.

7 Sew a white 2½" square to each end of each print 2½" × 8½" rectangle as shown. Make 25 units.

Make 25.

8 Sew a unit from step 6 between two matching units from step 5, rotating the units as shown. Make 50 units.

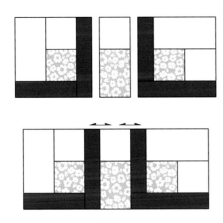

Make 50.

9 Sew a unit from step 7 between two matching units from step 8 to make a block as shown. Trim the block to 12½" square. Make 25 blocks.

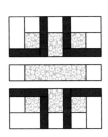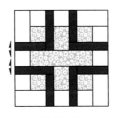

Make 25.

Assembling the Quilt Top

1 Lay out five rows of five blocks each as shown in the quilt layout diagram.

2 Sew the blocks together into rows, pressing the seam allowances open. Sew the rows together and press the seam allowances open.

3 Sew the green 6½" × 60½" strips to the sides of the quilt top. Press the seam allowances toward the borders. Sew the green 6½" × 72½" strips to the top and bottom of the quilt top. Press.

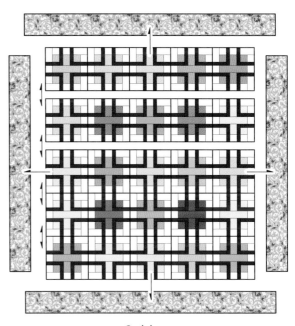

Quilt layout

Finishing the Quilt

Go to ShopMartingale.com/HowtoQuilt if you need more information on finishing techniques.

1 Layer and baste your quilt, and quilt as desired.

2 Using the coral 2½"-wide strips, prepare and attach the binding.

An Irish Braid

*Strip-pieced segments move liltingly across a light, airy field of white.
An intricately modern twist on the traditional Irish Chain pattern,
this design may quickly become one of your favorites.*

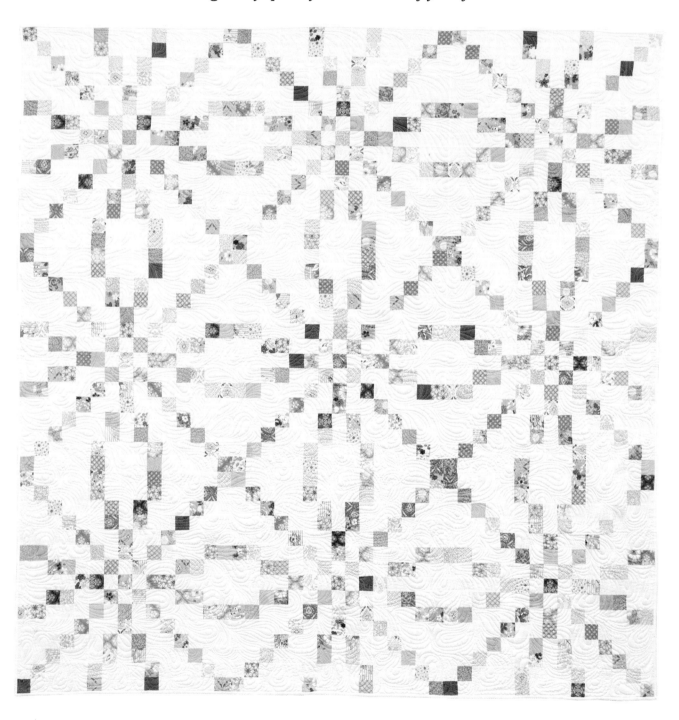

FINISHED QUILT: 90½" × 90½" • **FINISHED BLOCK:** 30" × 30"

Designed and made by Melissa Corry

Materials

Yardage is based on 42"-wide fabric.

40 precut strips, 2½" × 42", of assorted prints
   for blocks

6⅜ yards of white solid for block backgrounds

⅞ yard of fabric for binding

8½ yards of fabric for backing

100" × 100" piece of batting

Cutting

From the 40 print strips, crosscut *5 strips* into:

81 squares, 2½" × 2½"

From the white solid, cut:

62 strips, 2½" × 42"; crosscut *27 strips* into:
   144 rectangles, 2½" × 4½"
   36 rectangles, 2½" × 8½"

12 strips, 4½" × 42"; crosscut into 72 rectangles,
   4½" × 6½"

From the binding fabric, cut:

10 strips, 2½" × 42"

Making the Strip Units

Press the seam allowances as indicated by the arrows,
or as otherwise instructed.

1   Sew a print and a white 2½" × 42" strip together
    as shown. Make 35 strip sets. Cut 540 segments,
    2½" wide.

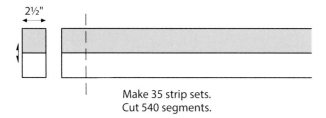

Make 35 strip sets.
Cut 540 segments.

2   Pin and sew two segments together to make a
    four-patch unit. Make 108 units.

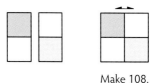

Make 108.

3   Pin and sew two segments from step 1 together,
    with the print squares adjoining. Make 144 one-
    sided four-patch units.

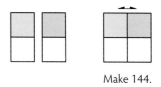

Make 144.

Making the A Blocks

1   Sew a four-patch unit and a white 4½" × 6½"
    rectangle together as shown. Make 72 side units.

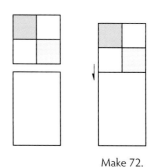

Make 72.

2   Pin and sew a print 2½" square between two
    white 2½" × 4½" rectangles. Make 36 center units.

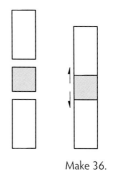

Make 36.

3 Pin and sew together two side units and one center unit as shown. Make 36 of block A.

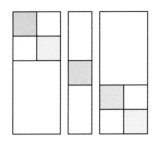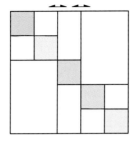

Block A.
Make 36.

//

THE DETAILS

Strip piecing really speeds up the construction of this quilt, but remember, you want accuracy as well as speed. There are a lot of seams to align. Here are a few tips that will help.

• Shorten the stitch length when sewing strip sets to keep cut stitches from coming undone.

• When pressing strip-pieced fabrics, take care to gently press the seam allowances open. It's very easy to stretch these long strips of fabric, especially when you've been pressing for a while and aren't paying attention.

• When you're ready to subcut the strip sets, you may be tempted to stack them to save time. But rather than stack them, spread them apart on your cutting mat. This way you can cut multiple strip sets at once, but you won't have any slipping where stacked seam allowances don't want to lie flat.

Making the B Blocks

1 Pin and sew together two one-sided four-patch units and a white 2½" × 4½" rectangle as shown. Make 36 left-side units.

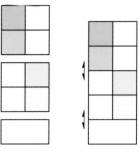

Make 36.

2 Pin and sew together two one-sided four-patch units and a white 2½" × 4½" rectangle as shown. Make 36 right-side units.

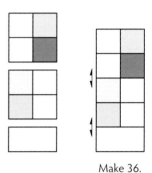

Make 36.

3 Sew a print 2½" square to a white 2½" × 8½" rectangle. Make 36 center units.

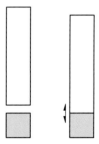

Make 36.

4 Pin and sew together a left-side unit, a center unit, and a right-side unit as shown. Make 36 of block B.

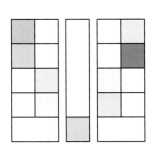 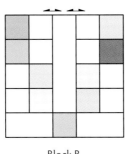

Block B.
Make 36.

3 Pin and sew together two side units and one center unit as shown. Make nine of block C.

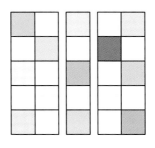 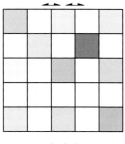

Block C.
Make 9.

Making the C Blocks

1 Pin and sew together two four-patch units and one strip-set segment so the print squares alternate. Make 18 side units.

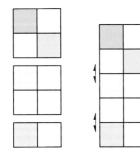

Make 18.

2 Sew together two strip-set segments and one print 2½" square so the print and white squares alternate. Make nine center units.

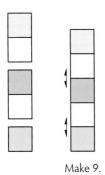

Make 9.

Making the ABC Blocks

1 Lay out four A blocks, four B blocks, and one C block in three vertical rows as shown.

2 Sew the blocks together into rows, press, and then sew the rows together. Make nine of block ABC.

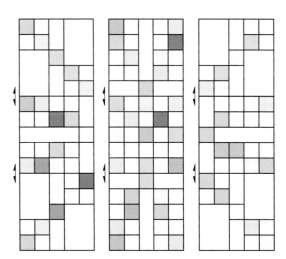

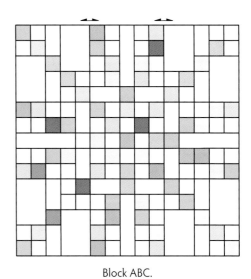

Block ABC.
Make 9.

Assembling the Quilt Top

1 Lay out the ABC blocks in three rows of three blocks each, referring to the quilt assembly diagram below.

2 Sew the blocks together into rows, and then sew the rows together. Press.

Finishing the Quilt

Go to ShopMartingale.com/HowtoQuilt if you need more information on finishing techniques.

1 Layer and baste your quilt, and quilt as desired.

2 Using the 2½"-wide binding strips, prepare and attach the binding.

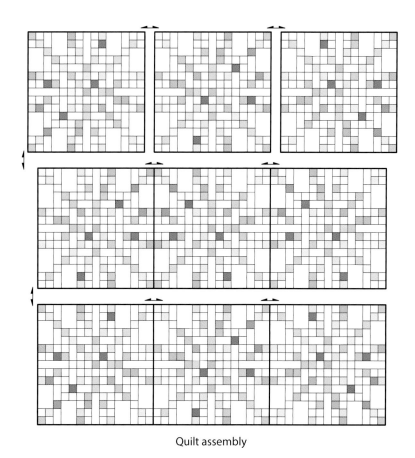

Quilt assembly

Rainbow Hearts

Cornelia Gauger proudly says, "I never met a color I didn't like!" Show off your own color crush, and if you can't bear to restrict the rainbow to just one side of the quilt, gather extra strips and make the back of the quilt as cheerful as the front.

FINISHED QUILT: 31¼" × 40½" • **FINISHED BLOCK:** 10" × 10"

Designed and pieced by Cornelia Gauger; machine quilted by Karen Burns of Compulsive Quilting

Materials

Yardage is based on 42"-wide fabric.

21 precut strips, 2½" × 42", of assorted bright tone on tones for blocks, cornerstones, border, and binding

1⅜ yards of white solid for setting triangles, sashing, and border

1½ yards of fabric for backing*

37" × 47" piece of batting

Or piece your backing from 2½" strips and scraps, as shown on page 31.

Cutting

From *each of 2* bright tone-on-tone strips, cut:
5 squares, 2½" × 2½" (10 total)
1 square, 1½" × 1½" (2 total)
1 strip, 2½" × 10" (2 total)

From *each of 19* bright tone-on-tone strips, cut:
1 strip, 2½" × 15" (19 total)
1 square, 2½" × 2½" (19 total; 5 are extra)
1 strip, 2½" × 10" (19 total; 1 is extra)

From the remainder of *each of 2* bright tone-on-tone strips, cut:
1 square, 1½" × 1½" (2 total)

From the white solid, cut:
3 strips, 2½" × 42"; crosscut into a *total* of:
   22 squares, 2½" × 2½"
   1 strip, 2½" × 15"
   4 rectangles, 2½" × 4"
3 squares, 7" × 7"; cut the squares in half diagonally to yield 6 triangles (1 is extra)
4 strips, 1½" × 42"; crosscut into a *total* of 12 strips, 1½" × 10½"
1 square, 15½" × 15½"; cut the square into quarters diagonally to yield 4 triangles
2 squares, 9⅜" × 9⅜"; cut the squares in half diagonally to yield 4 triangles
1 strip, 3½" × 42"
2 strips, 2" × 42"

Making the Blocks

Press the seam allowances as indicated by the arrows, or as otherwise instructed.

1. Draw a diagonal line from corner to corner on the wrong side of a white 2½" square. Place the square on a bright 2½" square, right sides together and raw edges aligned. Sew on the line. Trim ¼" from the line on one side and press. Repeat to make five half-square-triangle units using one bright color and five with a different bright color.

Make 5.   Make 5.

2. Create strip sets from the 19 bright 2½" × 15" strips and one white 2½" × 15" strip as shown. Cut five segments, 2½" wide, from each strip set.

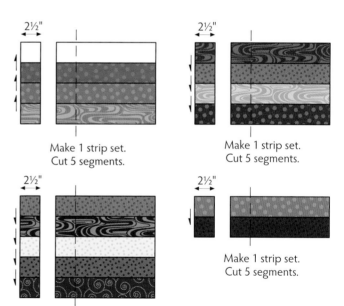

Make 1 strip set.
Cut 5 segments.

Make 1 strip set.
Cut 5 segments.

Make 1 strip set.
Cut 5 segments.

Make 2 strip sets.
Cut 5 segments from each (10 total).

3 Using one set of same-colored units from step 1, sew a half-square-triangle unit to one end of each two-square segment, angling the triangle seam as shown. Sew the remaining units from step 1 to the four-square segments, angling the triangle seam as shown.

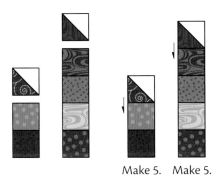

Make 5.   Make 5.

4 Arrange the units created in steps 2 and 3 as shown and sew them together to make the heart portion of the five blocks. Cornelia arranged the segments so all the blocks are identical. The seam allowances should butt, and you can match the seams without pinning, but if you're more comfortable pinning, feel free to do so.

5 Line up the ¼" line of a ruler along the junction of the squares on the top part of the heart and trim the squares as shown.

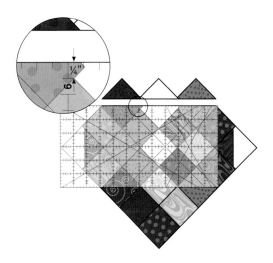

6 Find the center point of the top of the heart and the center point of the long side of the white 7" half-square triangles. Pin the centers and ends and sew. The ends of the triangle will extend past the heart. Sew with the pieced side on top so that you can make sure you're sewing directly over the points on the top row of the hearts. Be careful not to stretch the fabrics as you sew the bias edges together. Press the seam allowances toward the white triangle. Make five blocks. (You'll have one background triangle left over.)

Make 5 blocks.

7 Trim each block to 10½" square. The white triangles were cut slightly oversized to give you some wiggle room.

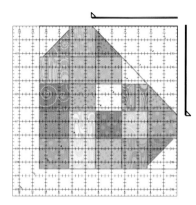

Assembling the Quilt Top

1 Arrange the blocks, 12 white 1½" × 10½" sashing strips, four bright 1½" squares for cornerstones, four white 15½" side setting triangles, and four white 9⅜" corner setting triangles. Sew the pieces together into rows, and then sew the rows together. Press the seam allowances open or in the directions shown.

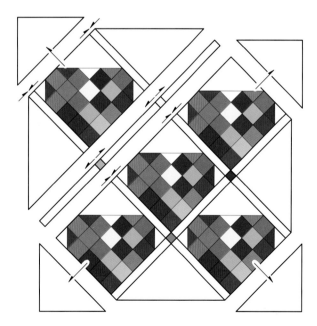

2 Line up the ¼" line of your ruler at the intersections of the top white triangles as shown and trim. Trim only the top edge of the quilt, not the sides or the bottom.

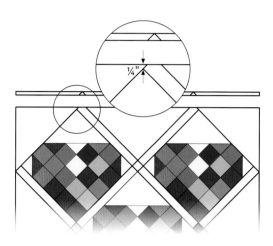

3 Measure the width of the quilt top through the center. Cut the white 3½" × 42" strip to this measurement and sew it to the bottom of the quilt top.

4 Sew seven of the remaining bright 2½" squares to six of the white 2½" squares as shown. Sew a white 2½" × 4" rectangle to each end to make a border unit. Sew a white 2" × 42" strip to one long side of the border unit. Press the seam allowances toward the white strip. Make two.

2½" x 4"   2½" x 4"

Make 2.

5 Measure evenly from the center of the middle bright squares to cut each border's length to the measurement from step 3. Sew the border units to the top and bottom of the quilt top. Press. Square up the sides of the quilt top.

Finishing the Quilt

Go to ShopMartingale.com/HowtoQuilt if you need more information on finishing techniques.

1 Layer and baste your quilt, and quilt as desired.

2 Using the bright 2½" × 10" strips, prepare and attach the binding.

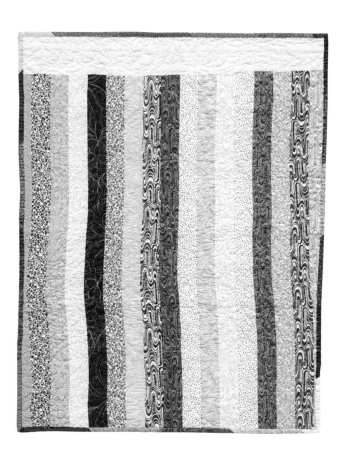

Pieced leftover 2½" strips give Rainbow Hearts a colorful backing.

Charleston

////////////

Civil War–era reproduction fabrics give this quilt an old-fashioned charm. If you don't have enough reproduction prints, substitute contemporary "look-alikes" to maintain the antique appearance.

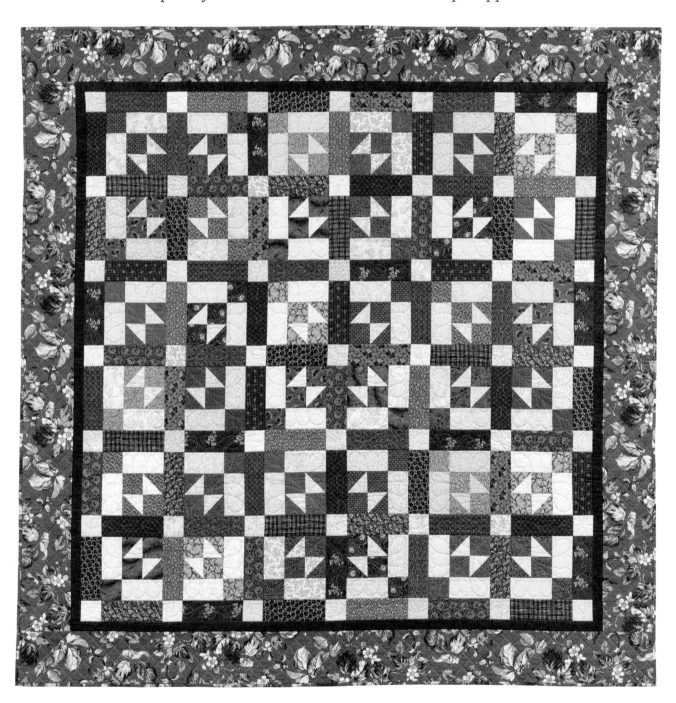

FINISHED QUILT: 62½" × 62½" • **FINISHED BLOCK:** 6" × 6"

Designed, pieced, and quilted by Kim Brackett

Materials

Yardage is based on 42"-wide fabric.

18 precut strips, 2½" × 42", of assorted beige prints for blocks and sashing squares

12 precut strips, 2½" × 42", of assorted pink prints for blocks

15 precut strips, 2½" × 42", of assorted brown prints for sashing

⅓ yard of brown print for inner border

1⅝ yards of large-scale floral for outer border and binding

4⅓ yards of fabric for backing

69" × 69" piece of batting

Cutting

From *each* of the 18 beige print strips, cut:
4 rectangles, 2½" × 4½" (72 total)
7 squares, 2½" × 2½" (126 total; 5 are extra)

From *each* of the 12 pink print strips, cut:
15 squares, 2½" × 2½" (180 total)

From *each* of the 15 brown print strips, cut:
6 rectangles, 2½" × 6½" (90 total; 6 are extra)

From the brown print for inner border, cut:
6 strips, 1½" × 42"

From the large-scale floral, cut:
6 strips, 5½" × 42"
7 strips, 2½" × 42"

CUTTING FROM YOUR STASH

Time to whittle down your fabric stash? To cut your blocks and sashing from scraps rather than using precut 2½" strips as listed in "Materials" at left, follow these instructions.

From assorted beige scraps, cut:
36 sets of:
- 2 rectangles, 2½" × 4½" (72 total)
- 2 squares, 2½" × 2½" (72 total)
49 squares, 2½" × 2½"

From assorted pink scraps, cut:
36 sets of 5 squares, 2½" × 2½" (180 total)

From assorted brown scraps, cut:
84 rectangles, 2½" × 6½"

Making the Blocks

Each block is made using the same pink print and the same beige print within the block. Press the seam allowances as indicated by the arrows, or as otherwise instructed.

1 Draw a diagonal line from corner to corner on the wrong side of a beige 2½" square. Place the marked square on a pink 2½" square, right sides together and raw edges aligned. Sew on the line. Trim ¼" from the line on one side and press. Make two for each block.

Make 2
for each block.

2 Sew a half-square-triangle unit to a pink 2½" square as shown. Make two for each block.

Make 2
for each block.

3 Sew together two of the units from step 2 as shown. Press the seam allowances in either direction.

4 Sew a beige 2½" × 4½" rectangle to the unit from step 3 as shown.

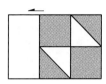

5 Sew a pink 2½" square to a beige 2½" × 4½" rectangle.

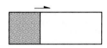

6 Sew together the units from steps 4 and 5 to complete one block. Make 36 blocks.

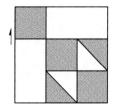

Make 36.

Assembling the Quilt Top

1 Lay out the blocks, the brown 2½" × 6½" rectangles, and the remaining beige 2½" squares as shown.

2 Sew the units together into rows; press. Sew the rows together and press the seam allowances in one direction.

3 Join the brown 1½"-wide strips end to end. Measure the length of the quilt top through the center. Cut two strips to that measurement and sew them to the sides of the quilt top. Press the seam allowances away from the center. Measure the width of the quilt top through the center, including the borders just added. Cut two strips to that measurement and sew them to the top and bottom of the quilt top to complete the inner border. Press the seam allowances away from the center.

4 Repeat with the floral 5½"-wide strips to add the outer border.

Finishing the Quilt

Go to ShopMartingale.com/HowtoQuilt if you need more information on finishing techniques.

1 Layer and baste your quilt, and quilt as desired.

2 Using the floral 2½"-wide strips, prepare and attach the binding.

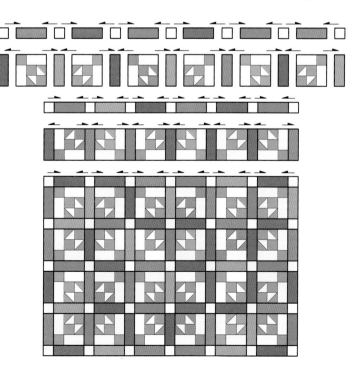

Plaid and Pinwheels

///////////////

The blocks in the center of this quilt have a hint-of-plaid appeal and are very quick to sew. The little blocks in the Pinwheel border will likely take longer—but aren't they precious?

FINISHED QUILT: 60½" × 84½" • **FINISHED BLOCK:** 10" × 10"

Designed and pieced by Nancy Allen; machine quilted by Sue Baddley

Materials

Yardage is based on 42"-wide fabric.

80 precut strips, 2½" × 42", of assorted red, beige, and blue prints for blocks and pieced second and fourth borders

1 yard of beige-and-blue print for sashing

⅔ yard of navy print for sashing cornerstones and first border

⅝ yard of red print for third border

⅔ yard of fabric for binding

5¼ yards of fabric for backing

69" × 93" piece of batting

1 package of 1½" triangle paper foundations (optional)

Cutting

From *each* of the 80 red, beige, and blue print strips, cut:

2 strips, 2½" × 21" (160 total)

From the beige-and-blue print, cut:

10 strips, 2½" × 42"; crosscut into 38 rectangles, 2½" × 10½"

From the navy print, cut:

8 strips, 2½" × 42"; crosscut *2 of the strips* into 24 squares, 2½" × 2½"

From the red print, cut:

7 strips, 2½" × 42"

From the binding fabric, cut:

8 strips, 2¼" × 42"

Organizing Your Fabrics

Each block uses three different fabrics: two for the four-patch units (fabrics A and B) and one for the rectangles (fabric C).

1. Mix and match 30 coordinated half strips into pairs until you have 15 pleasing fabric combinations for the four-patch units. Identify one fabric from each pair as fabric A and the other as fabric B. Select another half strip of each fabric A and cut a 2½" square from it for the block center square.

2. From the remaining strips, including the slightly shorter fabric A strips, select 15 strips that will become the rectangles in each block, fabric C. Pair these with the 15 combinations from step 1. Crosscut each fabric C strip into 4 rectangles, 2½" × 4½".

3. Reserve the remaining strips for the Pinwheel and checkerboard borders.

Making the Blocks

Press the seam allowances as indicated by the arrows, or as otherwise instructed.

1. Sew an A strip to a B strip along the length of the strips. Press the seam allowances toward the darker fabric. Crosscut the strip set into eight segments, 2½" wide.

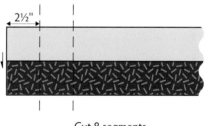

Cut 8 segments.

2. Join the two-patch units to make four-patch units with contrasting fabrics next to each other. Press the seam allowances to one side, or carefully clip the seam allowances at the intersection of the units, and clip up to, but not through, the stitching. Then press the seam allowances in either a clockwise or counterclockwise direction

so that the seams will oppose each other when you sew the blocks together.

Make 4.

3 Lay out the four-patch units, one 2½" square, and the four 2½" × 4½" rectangles for one block as shown. Sew the units into rows, and then sew the rows together to complete the block. The block should measure 10½" square. Make a total of 15 blocks.

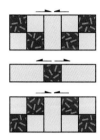 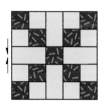

Make 15 blocks.

Assembling the Quilt Top

Refer to the quilt assembly diagram on page 39 as needed.

1 Lay out five rows of three blocks each. When you're happy with the arrangement, add four beige-and-blue 2½" × 10½" rectangles to the rows, alternating them with the blocks. Sew the blocks and sashing strips together in each row.

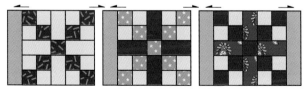

Make 5 rows.

2 Sew four navy 2½" squares and three beige-and-blue 2½" × 10½" rectangles together to make a sashing row. Make six rows.

Make 6.

3 Sew the six sashing rows together with the five block rows. Press the seam allowances toward the sashing rows. The quilt center should now measure 38½" × 62½".

Adding Borders

Refer to the quilt diagram on page 39 as you add the borders.

First Border

1 Sew six navy 2½" × 42" strips together end to end. Press the seam allowances open. Cut the pieced strip into two strips, 62½" long, and two strips, 42½" long.

2 Sew the 62½"-long strips to the sides of the quilt top, and sew the 42½"-long strips to the top and bottom to complete the border. The quilt top should now measure 42½" × 66½".

Second Border

1 Select 52 of the 2½" × 21" half strips and sort them into 26 pairs. Layer the strips right sides together and cut each pair into six layered 2½" squares. Draw a diagonal line from corner to corner on the wrong side of the lighter squares, keeping the squares aligned. Sew ¼" from the drawn line on both sides and cut on the line. Press the seam allowances toward the darker fabric. Make 76 sets of four matching half-square-triangle units (304 total). Trim and square up the units to measure 2" square. Nancy was able to get 12 half-square-triangle units from each pair of strips—enough for three Pinwheel blocks.

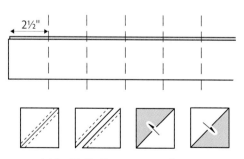

Make 304 half-square-triangle units.

2 Join four matching half-square-triangle units as shown to make a Pinwheel block that measures 3½" square. Carefully clip the seam allowances at the intersection of the units; clip up to, but not through, the stitching. Press the seam allowances either clockwise or counterclockwise. Make a total of 76 blocks.

Make 76.

3 Sew 22 Pinwheel blocks together side by side. Make two of these border strips and sew them to the sides of the quilt. Join 16 Pinwheel blocks in the same manner; make two. Sew these border strips to the top and bottom of the quilt. The quilt top should now measure 48½" × 72½".

Make 2 rows with 16 pinwheels.
Make 2 rows with 22 pinwheels.

Third Border

1 Join the seven red 2½" × 42" strips end to end. Press the seam allowances open. Cut the pieced strip into two strips, 72½" long, and two strips, 52½" long.

2 Sew the 72½"-long strips to the sides of the quilt top, and sew the 52½"-long strips to the top and bottom. The quilt top should now measure 52½" × 76½".

Fourth Border

1 Select 40 of the 2½" × 21" strips and sort them into 20 pairs. Sew each pair of strips together to make a strip set. Press the seam allowances toward the darker fabric. Crosscut the strip sets into 2½"-wide segments until you have a total of 136 two-patch units.

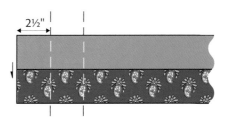

2½"

Make 20 strip sets.
Cut 136 segments.

2 Mix and match two-patch units and sew them into two borders with 38 two-patch units each and two borders with 30 two-patch units each. Alternate the direction of the light and dark fabrics to enhance the checkerboard design and permit the seam allowances to oppose each other.

Make 2 rows with 38 units.

Make 2 rows with 30 units.

3 Sew the longer border strips to the sides of the quilt top, and sew the shorter border strips to the top and bottom. The quilt top should now measure 60½" × 84½". Stay stitch around the outside of your quilt, about ⅛" in from the edge.

Finishing the Quilt

Go to ShopMartingale.com/HowtoQuilt if you need more information on finishing techniques.

1 Layer and baste your quilt, and quilt as desired.

2 Using the 2¼"-wide binding strips, prepare and attach the binding.

Quilt assembly

Snowball Explosion

These bright Striped Snowball blocks seem kissed by the sun. Good thing they're melt-proof! The blocks are easy to make, and the strip piecing creates a secondary pattern that rises above the ordinary.

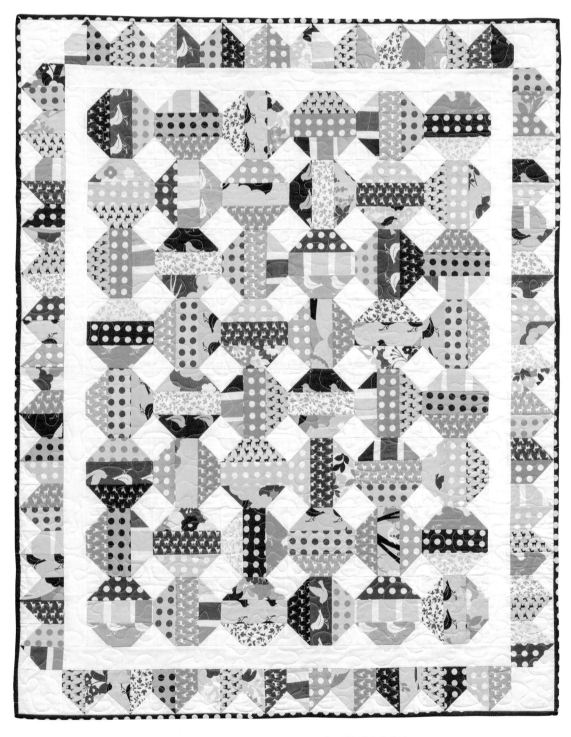

FINISHED QUILT: 48" × 60" • **FINISHED BLOCK:** 6" × 6"

Designed, pieced, and quilted by Kate Henderson

Materials

Yardage is based on 42"-wide fabric.

40 precut strips, 2½" × 42", of assorted bright prints for blocks and borders

1⅞ yards of white solid for blocks and borders

½ yard of brown print for binding

3 yards of fabric for backing

54" × 66" piece of batting

Cutting

From *each* of 36 bright print strips, cut:

1 strip, 2½" × 27" (36 total)

2 rectangles, 2½" × 4½" (72 total)

From *each* of 4 bright print strips, cut:

5 rectangles, 2½" × 4½" (20 total)

From the white solid, cut:

24 strips, 2½" × 42"; crosscut *19 strips* into 284 squares, 2½" × 2½"

1 strip, 4½" × 42"; crosscut into 4 squares, 4½" × 4½"

From the brown print, cut:

6 strips, 2½" × 42"

Making the Blocks

Press the seam allowances as indicated by the arrows, or as otherwise instructed.

1 Organize the 2½" × 27" strips into 12 piles of three strips each. Sew each group of strips together along their long edges. Cut four 6½" squares from each strip set.

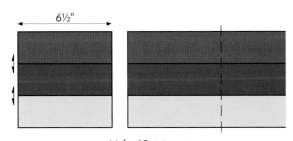

Make 12 strip sets.
Cut 4 squares from each.

2 Draw a diagonal line from corner to corner on the wrong side of four white 2½" squares. Place a marked square on each corner of a pieced square as shown, right sides together and corners aligned. Sew on the lines. Trim the excess corner fabric, leaving a ¼" seam allowance, and press. Repeat to make 48 blocks.

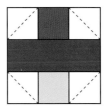 

Make 48.

Assembling the Quilt Top

1 Lay out eight rows of six blocks each, rotating every other block as shown in the quilt assembly diagram below.

2 Sew the blocks together into rows, and then sew the rows together.

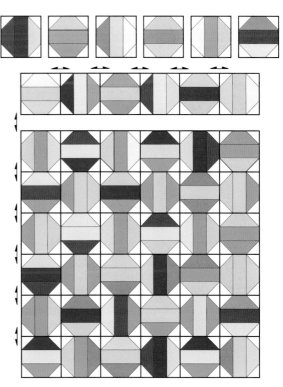

Quilt assembly

3 Join three white 2½" × 42" strips end to end. From the pieced strip, cut two strips, 48½" long. Trim each of the two remaining white 2½" × 42" strips to 40½" long. Sew the 48½"-long strips to the sides of the quilt top, and sew the 40½"-long strips to the top and bottom to complete the inner border.

4 Referring to the technique used in step 2 of "Making the Blocks" on page 41, place a marked white 2½" square on one end of a print rectangle. Stitch, trim, and press. Make 46 each of units A and B.

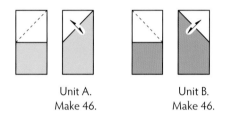

Unit A.
Make 46.

Unit B.
Make 46.

5 Sew the A and B units together in pairs as shown.

6 Sew 13 of the units from step 5 together to make two side borders. Sew 10 units together, and add a white 4½" square to each end. Make two for the top and bottom borders.

7 Sew the pieced side borders to the quilt top and then add the pieced top and bottom borders.

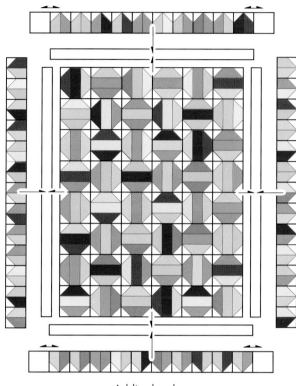

Adding borders

Finishing the Quilt

Go to ShopMartingale.com/HowtoQuilt if you need more information on finishing techniques.

1 Layer and baste your quilt, and quilt as desired.

2 Using the brown 2½"-wide strips, prepare and attach the binding.

Roll of Stamps

Several variations of the Postage Stamp block have been introduced throughout the years. Some versions, like this one, use the conventional style of block construction but alter the color placement. To make your quilt more traditional, use just two fabrics per block and alternate the colors.

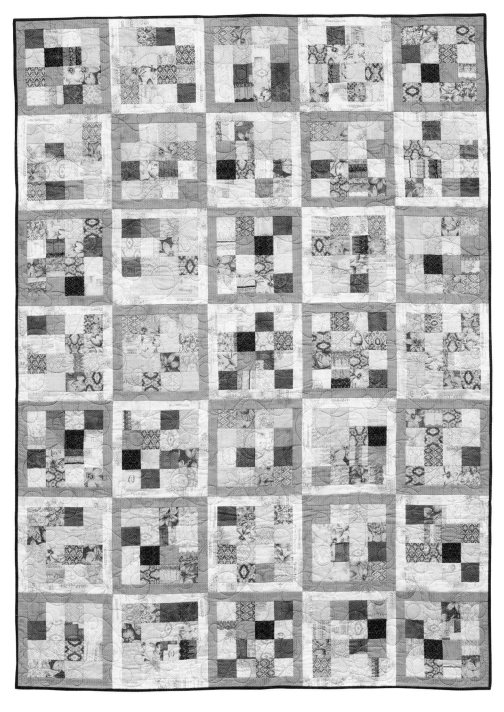

FINISHED QUILT: 50½" × 70½" • **FINISHED BLOCK:** 10" × 10"

Designed, pieced, and quilted by Rebecca Silbaugh

Materials

Yardage is based on 42"-wide fabric.
36 precut strips, 2½" × 42", of assorted prints
  for blocks
⅞ yard of white print for blocks
⅞ yard of green print for blocks
⅝ yard of brown print for binding
3½ yards of fabric for backing
58" × 78" piece of batting

Cutting

From *each* of the 36 print strips, cut:
2 strips, 2½" × 20" (72 total)

From the white print, cut:
17 strips, 1½" × 42"; crosscut *each* strip into:
  2 rectangles, 1½" × 8½" (34 total)
  2 rectangles, 1½" × 10½" (34 total)

From the green print, cut:
18 strips, 1½" × 42"; crosscut *each* strip into:
  2 rectangles, 1½" × 8½" (36 total)
  2 rectangles, 1½" × 10½" (36 total)

From the brown print, cut:
7 strips, 2¼" × 42"

Making the Blocks

Press the seam allowances as indicated by the arrows,
or as otherwise instructed.

1 Randomly select four 2½"-wide strips and sew
  them together in pairs along the long edges.
  Join the pairs to make a strip set. Make 18 strip
  sets. Crosscut the strip sets into a total of 140
  segments, 2½" wide.

Make 18 strip sets.
Cut 140 segments.

2 Randomly select four segments from step 1.
  With the previously sewn seam allowances in
  alternating directions, sew the segments together.
  Make 35 units.

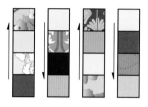 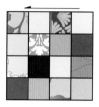

Make 35.

3 Sew white 1½" × 8½" rectangles to the sides
  of 17 units from step 2. Sew white 1½" × 10½"
  rectangles to the top and bottom of these units
  to complete the white blocks. Repeat to sew the
  green rectangles to the remaining units from step
  2 to make 18 green blocks. Each block should
  measure 10½" square.

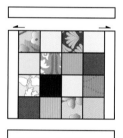

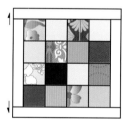 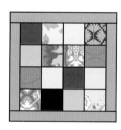

Make 17.   Make 18.

BUILDING A STRIP STASH

Instead of cutting all your leftover fabrics from
other projects into squares or small pieces, cut
some scraps into strips. By cutting remnants into
2½" × 42" strips, over time you can make your
own roll of strips for a one-of-a-kind collection!

Assembling the Quilt Top

1 Lay out seven rows of five blocks each, alternating the white and green blocks in each row and from row to row. To avoid having to match seams from block to block, position the longest rectangles of the green blocks so they run horizontally and the longest rectangles of the white blocks so they run vertically.

2 When you're pleased with the placement of fabrics and colors, sew the blocks in each row together, pressing the seam allowances toward the green blocks. Sew the rows together and press the seam allowances away from the center row.

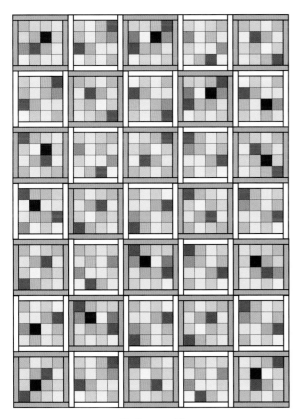

Quilt assembly

QUILTS WITHOUT BORDERS

There isn't a rule, written or otherwise, that requires borders on every quilt. If you'd like to add them, go for it! If you think the quilt is fine without, don't fix what's not broken!

Finishing the Quilt

Go to ShopMartingale.com/HowtoQuilt if you need more information on finishing techniques.

1 Layer and baste your quilt, and quilt as desired.

2 Using the brown 2¼"-wide strips, prepare and attach the binding.

Forties Four Patch

//////////////

Showcase a collection of 1930s and '40s reproduction fabrics with this Four Patch block. The block is made in two color combinations, reversing the light and dark fabrics, which creates the chain pattern that dances across the quilt.

FINISHED QUILT: 60½" × 76½" • **FINISHED BLOCK:** 8" × 8"

Designed and pieced by Nancy J. Martin; quilted by Frankie Schmitt

Materials

Yardage is based on 42"-wide fabric. Fat quarters are 18" × 21".

8 strips, 2½" × 22", of assorted red prints for blocks
8 strips, 2½" × 22", of assorted blue prints for blocks
8 strips, 2½" × 22", of assorted lavender prints
    for blocks
24 strips, 2½" × 22", of assorted white tone on tones
    for blocks
6 fat quarters, 2 *each* of red, blue, and lavender prints
    for blocks
4 fat quarters of white tone on tones for blocks
½ yard of white print for inner border
1 yard of red print for outer border
⅝ yard of blue print for bias binding
3⅞ yards of fabric for backing
69" × 85" piece of batting

Cutting

From *each* of the 6 red, blue, and lavender fat quarters, cut:
8 squares, 4½" × 4½" (48 total, 16 of each color)

From *each* of the 4 white fat quarters, cut:
12 squares, 4½" × 4½" (48 total)

From the white print for inner border, cut:
6 strips, 2½" × 42"

From the red print for outer border, cut:
7 strips, 4½" × 42"

From the blue print for binding, cut:
282" of 2¼"-wide bias strips

Making the Blocks

You will make two color combinations of this block, one with white 4½" squares and one with random pairings of red, blue, and lavender print 4½" squares. Press the seam allowances as indicated by the arrows, or as otherwise instructed.

1 Make the four-patch units by stitching each white 2½" × 22" strip to a red, blue, or lavender strip to make 24 strip sets.

Make 24 strip sets.

2 Layer two sets of strips right sides together, with the dark and light strips facing each other as shown. Cut each layered pair of strip sets into eight segments, 2½" wide (192 total).

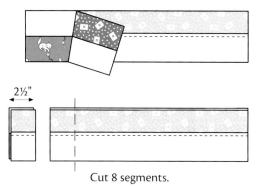

2½"

Cut 8 segments.

3 Stitch the segments together to make 96 four-patch units.

Make 96.

4 Combine two four-patch units with two print 4½" squares to make 24 dark blocks.

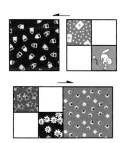
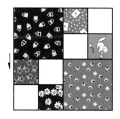

Make 24.

5 Combine two four-patch units with two white 4½" squares to make 24 light blocks.

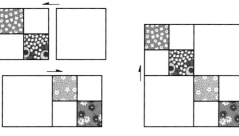

Make 24.

Assembling the Quilt Top

1 Lay out eight rows of six blocks each, alternating the dark and light blocks as shown in the quilt assembly diagram below.

2 Sew the blocks in each row together; press. Sew the rows together and press the seam allowances in one direction.

Quilt assembly

3 Join the white 2½"-wide strips end to end. Measure the length of the quilt top through the center. Cut two strips to that measurement and sew them to the sides of the quilt top. Press the seam allowances away from the center. Measure the width of the quilt top through the center, including the side borders just added. Cut two strips to that measurement and sew them to the top and bottom of the quilt top to complete the inner border. Press the seam allowances away from the center.

4 Repeat to add the red 4½"-wide strips for the outer border.

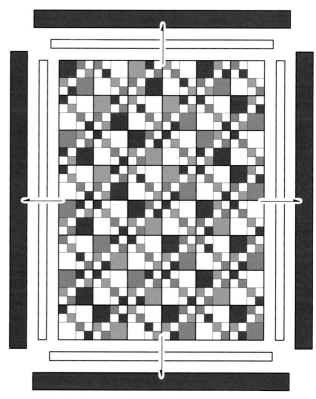

Adding borders

Finishing the Quilt

Go to ShopMartingale.com/HowtoQuilt if you need more information on finishing techniques.

1 Layer and baste your quilt, and quilt as desired.

2 Using the blue 2¼"-wide bias strips, prepare and attach the binding.

My Garden Trellis

A Stacked Coin quilt is a perfect outlet for using up scraps, and easy piecing is an added bonus! This fun project would make an excellent beginner quilt or a quick, smile-inducing gift for a charitable cause.

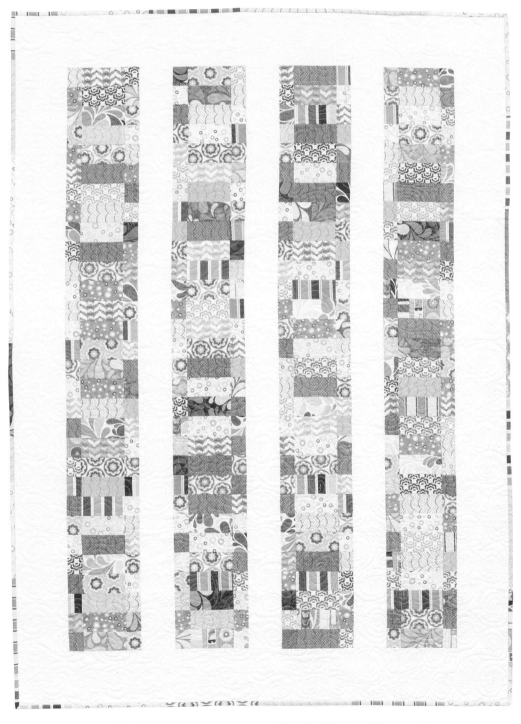

FINISHED QUILT: 54" × 71½" • **FINISHED BLOCK:** 8" × 12"

Designed, pieced, and quilted by Sue Pfau

Materials

Yardage is based on 42"-wide fabric.

30 to 35 precut strips, 2½" × 42", of assorted prints for blocks

2 yards of white fabric for sashing and border

⅝ yard of fabric for binding*

3½ yards of fabric for backing

62" × 80" piece of batting

Or 7 precut strips, 2½" × 42", of assorted prints for a scrappy binding

Cutting

From the 30 to 35 print strips, cut a *total* of:

120 strips, 2½" × 10"

From the white fabric, cut on the *lengthwise* grain*:

3 strips, 4" × length of fabric

4 strips, 6" × length of fabric

From the binding fabric, cut:

7 strips, 2½" × 42"

You will trim the sashing and border strips to fit after your quilt blocks have been pieced.

Making the Blocks

Press the seam allowances as indicated by the arrows, or as otherwise instructed.

1 Sew six 2½" × 10" strips together along the long edges. When sewing the strip sets together, try to mix a variety of colors and prints in each set. Make 20 strip sets.

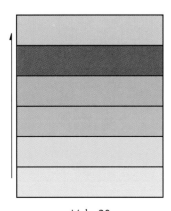

Make 20 strip sets.

2 Cut each strip set into one 5½"-wide segment and two 2"-wide segments.

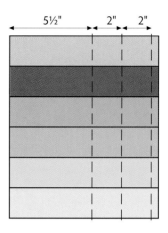

3 Sew random 2"-wide segments to opposite sides of a 5½"-wide segment. Nest the seam allowances together so the corners match up nicely. Press. Make 20 blocks.

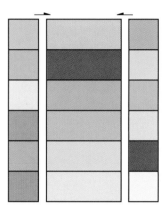

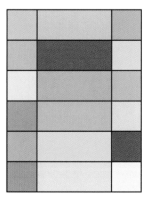

Make 20.

Assembling the Quilt Top

1. Lay out four vertical rows of five blocks each. Sew the blocks into vertical rows and press the seam allowances in one direction.

2. Measure the length of the rows and determine the average measurement; it should be 60½". Trim the three white 4"-wide strips and two of the white 6"-wide strips to the same average length of the vertical rows.

3. Sew the vertical block rows together with the 4"-wide sashing strips.

4. Sew the white 6"-wide border strips from step 2 to the sides of the quilt top.

5. Measure the width of the quilt top through the center; it should be 54". Trim the remaining white 6"-wide border strips to this measurement, and sew them to the top and bottom of the quilt top.

Finishing the Quilt

Go to ShopMartingale.com/HowtoQuilt if you need more information on finishing techniques.

1. Layer and baste your quilt, and quilt as desired.

2. Using the 2½"-wide binding strips, prepare and attach the binding.

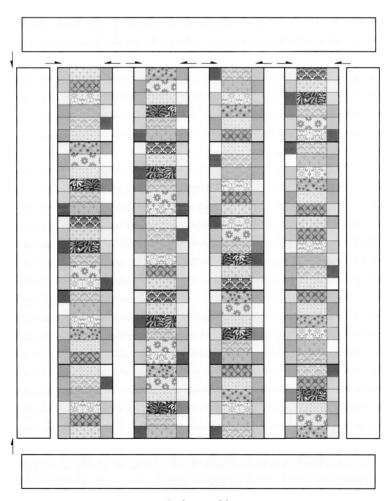

Quilt assembly

A Little Tangy

When designer Kim Brackett showed this quilt to her husband to elicit his comments, he declared it to be "a little tangy" for his taste. The palette might not suit every palate, but if zing is your thing, this one's for you!

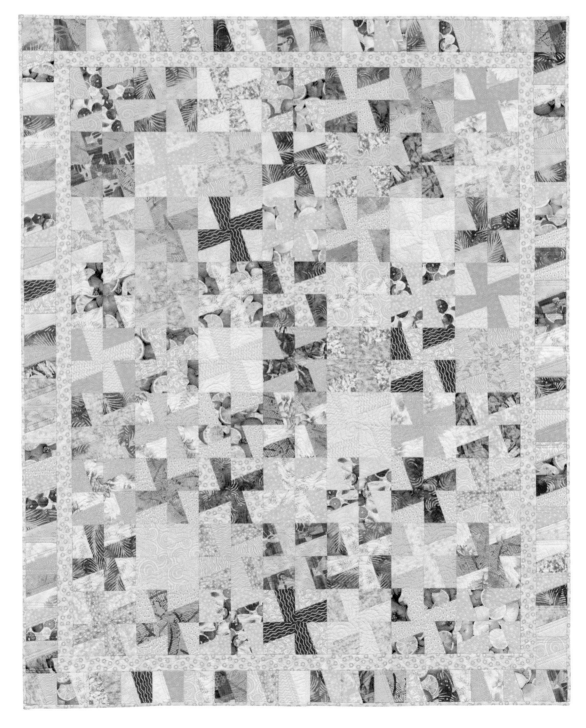

FINISHED QUILT: 51½" × 63½" • **FINISHED BLOCK:** 6" × 6"

Designed, pieced, and quilted by Kim Brackett

Materials

Yardage is based on 42"-wide fabric.

66 precut strips, 2½" × 42", of assorted yellow, orange, and green prints for blocks and pieced outer border

1 yard of yellow print for inner border and binding

3¾ yards of fabric for backing

58" × 70" piece of batting

Cutting

From the yellow print for border and binding, cut:

6 strips, 2" × 42"

7 strips, 2½" × 42"

CUTTING FROM YOUR STASH

For a different approach that will reduce your fabric stash, build your quilt one block at a time. Rather than collect 66 precut strips for the entire quilt, for each block (four units), cut two contrasting 2½" × 18" strips.

Making the Blocks

The edges of every piece in this quilt will be cut on the bias, requiring extra care when handling so that the quilt doesn't stretch out of shape. If you're cutting your own 2½" strips from your stash, you may find it helpful to use spray starch on your fabrics before cutting the strips. If you're using precut strips, spray them with starch *after* sewing the strips together in pairs. Once the blocks are cut, press only the seam allowances, avoiding touching the iron on the outside edges of the blocks. Press the seam allowances as indicated by the arrows, or as otherwise instructed.

1 Sew two contrasting 2½" × 42" strips together along the long edges, extending the bottom strip by ½" as shown. Press the seam allowances in either direction. Make 33 strip sets.

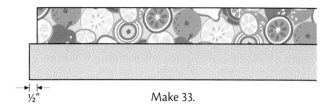

½"   Make 33.

2 Trace or photocopy the cutting pattern on page 55. Cut out the paper template around the outside edges. It should be 3½" square. Tape the template right side up to the bottom corner of a 6½"-square ruler (or any ruler with a 3½" mark). Place the ruler on the strip set so the line in the middle of the template follows the seamline on the strip set. Cut along the right and top edges of the ruler. Rotate the cut piece to trim the edges as shown, placing the previously cut edges along the edge of the template. Cut along the right and top edges of the ruler. Cut 10 of these units from each strip set.

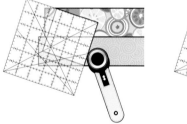 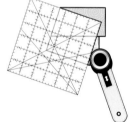

Cut 10 from each strip set.

3 From 31 of the strip sets, use 8 of 10 matching units to construct pairs of blocks, with the fabric placement in one block the reverse of the other as shown. Carefully clip the seam allowances at the intersection of the units; clip up to, but not

through, the stitching. Press the seam allowances in a counterclockwise direction. Construct a single block from one of the strip sets to make a total of 63 blocks. Set aside the leftover units for the outer border (six of the units will not be used).

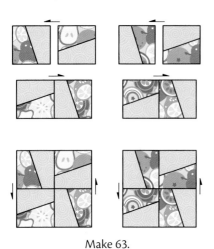

Make 63.

Assembling the Quilt Top

1 Lay out nine rows of seven blocks each.

2 Sew the blocks together into rows; press. Sew the rows together and press the seam allowances in one direction.

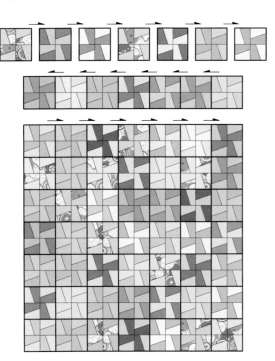

3 Join the yellow 2"-wide strips end to end. Cut two strips, 54½" long, and two strips, 45½" long. Sew the 54½"-long strips to the sides of the quilt top. Press the seam allowances toward the border. Join the 45½"-long strips to the top and bottom of the quilt top to complete the inner border. Press the seam allowances toward the border.

4 Join 19 leftover pieced units for each of the side borders and join 17 leftover pieced units for each of the top and bottom borders. Press the seam allowances to one side. Sew the pieced side borders to the quilt top, and then sew the pieced top and bottom borders.

Finishing the Quilt

Go to ShopMartingale.com/HowtoQuilt if you need more information on finishing techniques.

1 Layer and baste your quilt, and quilt as desired.

2 Using the yellow 2½"-wide strips, prepare and attach the binding.

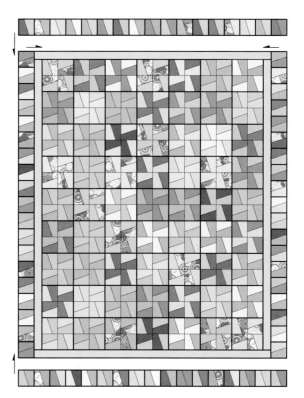

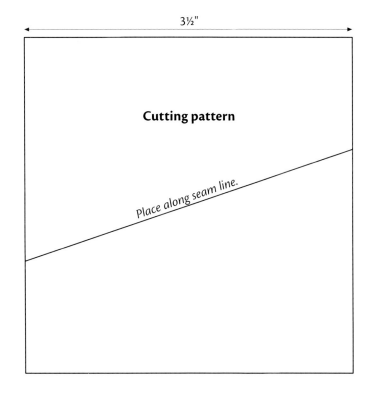

3½"

Cutting pattern

Place along seam line.

Jelly Fish

Inspired by a trip to the aquarium with her grandson, designer Virginia Lauth has captured the vibrant world of the fish in their tanks as well as the pure delight that results when we see everything around us through a child's eyes.

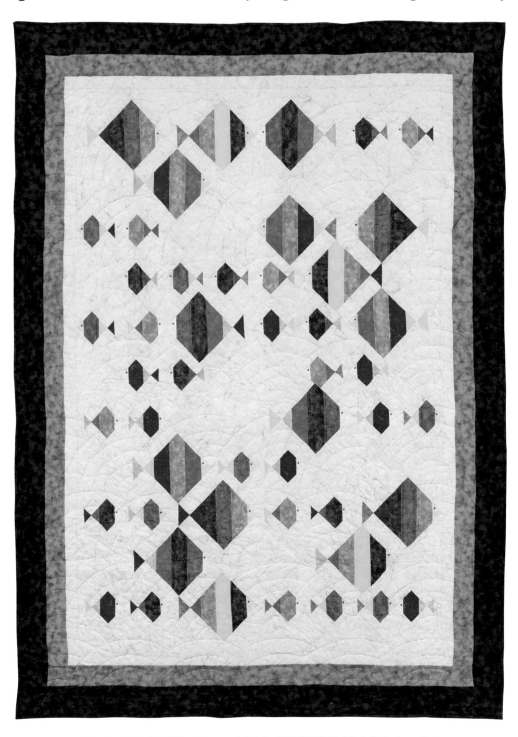

FINISHED QUILT: 59¾" × 82½" • **FINISHED BLOCK:** 8" × 8"

Designed, pieced, and hand quilted by Virginia Lauth

Materials

Yardage is based on 42"-wide fabric.

8 precut strips, 2½" × 42", of assorted yellow and yellow-green prints for fish faces

28 precut strips, 2½" × 42", of assorted bright prints for fish bodies and tails

3⅛ yards of light blue print for background, setting pieces, and inner border

¾ yard of turquoise print for middle border

1½ yards of dark blue print for outer border and binding

5¼ yards of fabric for backing

66" × 89" piece of batting

8" Bias Square® or other square ruler

48 small black beads for eyes (optional)

Blue water-soluble marker (optional)

Cutting

From *each* of 4 bright print strips, cut:

4 squares, 2½" × 2½" (16 total)

8 squares, 1¾" × 1¾" (32 total)

From the light blue print, cut:

4 squares, 12⅝" × 12⅝"; cut the squares into quarters diagonally to yield 16 triangles

2 squares, 6⅝" × 6⅝"; cut the squares in half diagonally to yield 4 triangles

2 strips, 8½" × 42"; crosscut into 7 squares, 8½" × 8½"

4 strips, 4½" × 42"; crosscut into 32 squares, 4½" × 4½"

2 strips, 6½" × 42"; crosscut into 32 rectangles, 2½" × 6½"

3 strips, 3¼" × 42"; crosscut into 64 rectangles, 1¾" × 3¼"

1 strip, 2½" × 42"; crosscut into 16 squares, 2½" × 2½"

2 strips, 1¾" × 42"; crosscut into 32 squares, 1¾" × 1¾"

6 strips, 1½" × 42"

From the turquoise print, cut:

7 strips, 3" × 42"

From the dark blue print, cut:

7 strips, 4" × 42"

8 strips, 2½" × 42"

Making the Large Fish Blocks

Press the seam allowances as indicated by the arrows, or as otherwise instructed.

1 Sew together four bright 2½" × 42" strips and one yellow or yellow-green 2½" × 42" strip. Be sure that the yellow strip, which will be the fish face, is on an outer edge. The other four strip colors can be arranged randomly. Make four strip sets.

Make 4 strip sets.

2 Mark a center lengthwise through the middle strip of each strip set, either by using a water-soluble marker or by pressing a crease. Align the center line of the Bias Square ruler with the marked line and cut 16 bias squares, 6½" × 6½". Make the cuts as shown, rotating the ruler 180° after making the first two cuts. Each strip set will yield four squares. Handle the squares carefully as the edges will be on the bias.

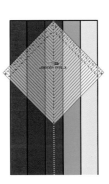 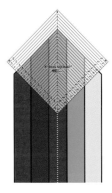

Align center of square with center of strip set.   Cut 16 squares, 6½" × 6½".

3 To make the tail units, pair one light blue 2½" square with one bright 2½" square, right sides together. Draw a diagonal line from corner to corner on the wrong side of the light blue square. Sew the squares together on the line. Trim ¼" from the line on one side and press the seam allowances toward the darker triangle. Make 16 tail units measuring 2½" square.

Make 16.

4 Using one 6½" bias square, one tail unit, and two light blue 2½" × 6½" rectangles, assemble the block as shown. Be sure that the yellow face and the tail unit are on opposite corners. Avoid stretching when attaching the rectangles to the bias edges of the fish bodies. Make 16 large fish blocks, pressing seam allowances open.

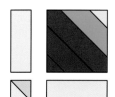 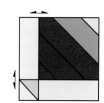

Make 16.

Making the Small Fish Blocks

1 Sew together one yellow or yellow-green 2½" × 42" strip and two bright 2½" × 42" strips. Be sure that the yellow strip is on the outer edge. The remaining two strip colors can be placed in any order. Make four strip sets.

Make 4 strip sets.

2 Repeat step 2 of "Making the Large Fish Blocks" on page 57 to mark a center line lengthwise through the middle strip of each strip set and

cut 32 bias squares, 3¼" × 3¼". Each strip set will yield eight squares.

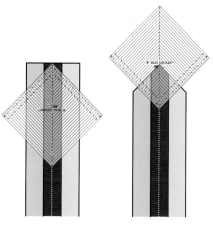

Align center of square with center of strip set.

Cut 32 squares, 3¼" × 3¼".

3 To make the tail units, repeat step 3 of "Making the Large Fish Blocks" using one light blue 1¾" square and one bright 1¾" square for each. Make 32.

4 Using two bias squares, two tail units, four light blue 1¾" × 3¼" rectangles, and two light blue 4½" squares, assemble the block as shown. For each fish, be sure that the yellow face and the tail unit are on opposite corners. Take care when adding the rectangles and background squares so that you do not stretch the bias edges of the fish bodies. Make 16 blocks as shown, pressing seam allowances open.

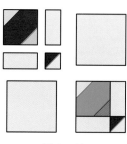

Make 14.

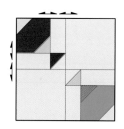

Make 1.

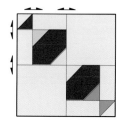

Make 1.

Assembling the Quilt Top

1 Lay out the fish blocks and light blue 8½" squares in diagonal rows, placing the large and small fish randomly and alternating the direction of some of the blocks to group the fish into schools as desired. Add the side and corner triangles, referring to the quilt diagram.

2 Sew the blocks together into rows, taking care not to stretch the bias edges of the fish bodies. Sew the rows together and add the corner triangles last. Press seam allowances open.

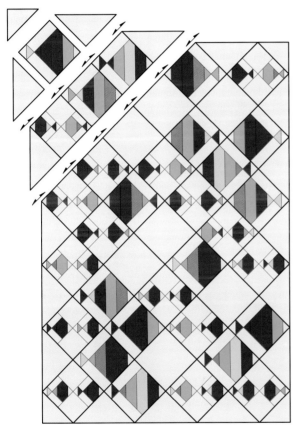

Quilt assembly

3 Join the light blue 1½"-wide strips end to end. Measure the length of the quilt top through the center. Cut two strips to that measurement and sew them to the sides of the quilt top. Press the seam allowances away from the center. Measure the width of the quilt top through the center, including the borders just added. Cut two strips to that measurement and sew them to the top and bottom of the quilt top to complete the inner border. Press.

4 Repeat with the turquoise 3"-wide strips to add the middle border.

5 Repeat with the dark blue 4"-wide strips to add the outer border.

Finishing the Quilt

Go to ShopMartingale.com/HowtoQuilt if you need more information on finishing techniques.

1 Layer and baste your quilt, and quilt as desired.

2 Using the dark blue 2½"-wide strips, prepare and attach the binding.

3 Sew on the black beads for eyes, or embroider them if the quilt is for a younger child.

That '70s Quilt

////////////

These colors have a quirky retro vibe, but when a simple quilt block is set on point, the look is new and decidedly fresh.

FINISHED QUILT: 68" × 68" • **FINISHED BLOCK:** 10" × 10"

Designed, pieced, and quilted by Kate Henderson

Materials

Yardage is based on 42"-wide fabric.

38 precut strips, 2½" × 42", of assorted bold prints
   for blocks and setting pieces
3 yards of white solid for background
¾ yard of black print for binding
4⅜ yards of fabric for backing
74" × 74" piece of batting

Cutting

From *each* of 25 bold print strips, cut:

2 rectangles, 2½" × 10½" (50 total)
2 rectangles, 2½" × 6½" (50 total)
2 squares, 2½" × 2½" (50 total)

From *each* of 13 bold print strips, cut:

4 rectangles, 2½" × 6½" (52 total; 2 are extra)
5 squares, 2½" × 2½" (65 total)

From the white solid, cut:

24 strips, 2½" × 42"; crosscut into:
   64 rectangles, 2½" × 10½"
   100 squares, 2½" × 2½"
2 strips, 15⅜" × 42"; crosscut into 3 squares,
   15⅜" × 15⅜". Cut the squares into quarters
   diagonally to yield 12 triangles.
1 strip, 8" × 42"; crosscut into 2 squares, 8" × 8". Cut
   the squares in half diagonally to yield 4 triangles.

From the black print, cut:

8 strips, 2½" × 42"

Making the Blocks

Press the seam allowances as indicated by the arrows,
or as otherwise instructed.

1 Sew matching print squares to the top and
bottom of a contrasting print square.

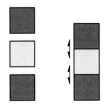

2 Sew 2½" × 6½" rectangles that match the outer
squares to both sides of the unit from step 1.

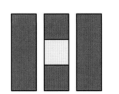

3 Sew matching 2½" × 6½" rectangles that contrast
with the rest of the block to the top and bottom of
the unit from step 2.

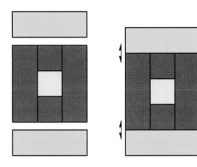

4 Draw a diagonal line from corner to corner on
the wrong side of the white 2½" squares. Select
a print 2½" × 10½" rectangle that matches those
added in step 3 and place a marked square on
each end of the rectangle as shown, right sides
together and corners aligned. Sew on the lines.
Trim the excess corner fabric, leaving a ¼" seam
allowance, and press. Make two matching units.

5 Sew the units from step 4 to opposite sides of the
unit from step 3, orienting the triangles as shown.
Make 25.

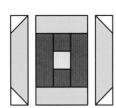 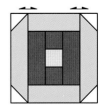

Make 25.

Assembling the Quilt Top

1 Trim 16 of the remaining print squares ¼" from the diagonal centerline of the square as shown.

2 Arrange the blocks, white rectangles, setting triangles, remaining print squares, and print triangles from step 1 as shown in the quilt assembly diagram below.

3 Sew the pieces together in diagonal rows, and then sew the rows together, adding the corner triangles last.

Finishing the Quilt

Go to ShopMartingale.com/HowtoQuilt if you need more information on finishing techniques.

1 Layer and baste your quilt, and quilt as desired.

2 Using the black 2½"-wide strips, prepare and attach the binding.

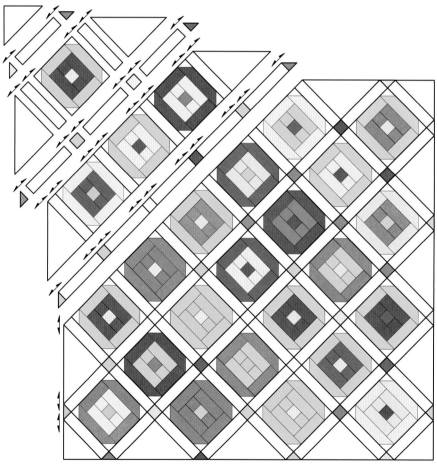

Quilt assembly

Boxed In

Strips of pink and off-white fabric frame these blocks sweetly, while a dynamic on-point setting creates a show-stopping quilt that isn't shy about grabbing your attention.

FINISHED QUILT: 51½" × 51½" • **FINISHED BLOCK:** 12" × 12"

Designed and pieced by Julie Herman; machine quilted by Angela Walters

Materials

Yardage is based on 42"-wide fabric.
25 precut strips, 2½" × 42", of assorted prints
    for blocks
⅞ yard of pink print for blocks
1 yard of off-white print for blocks
½ yard of light stripe for binding
3½ yards of fabric for backing
57" × 57" piece of batting

Cutting

From the 25 print strips, cut a *total* of:
384 squares, 2½" × 2½"

From the pink print, cut:
18 strips, 1½" × 42"; crosscut into:
    18 rectangles, 1½" × 12½"
    18 rectangles, 1½" × 10½"
    18 rectangles, 1½" × 6½"
    18 rectangles, 1½" × 4½"

From the off-white print, cut:
20 strips, 1½" × 42"; crosscut into:
    20 rectangles, 1½" × 12½"
    8 rectangles, 1½" × 11½"
    8 rectangles, 1½" × 10½"
    20 rectangles, 1½" × 6½"
    8 rectangles, 1½" × 5½"
    8 rectangles, 1½" × 4½"

From the light stripe, cut:
6 strips, 2½" × 42"

Making the Blocks

This is a one-block quilt in which fabric placement creates the illusion of a two-block design. Directions are included for making partial blocks to save fabric and time. However, if you prefer to make full blocks instead of partial blocks, additional fabric will be needed. Press the seam allowances as indicated by the arrows, or as otherwise instructed.

Making the Full Blocks

1   Lay out four assorted squares in a four-patch arrangement as shown. Join the squares to complete the four-patch unit.

2   Sew pink 1½" × 4½" rectangles to opposite sides of the four-patch unit. Then sew pink 1½" × 6½" rectangles to the top and bottom of the unit.

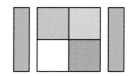 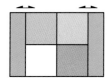

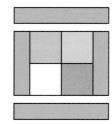 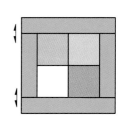

3   Select six assorted squares. Join them in groups of three to make two 6½"-long strips.

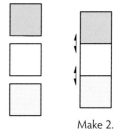

Make 2.

4 Sew the strips from step 3 to opposite sides of the unit from step 2.

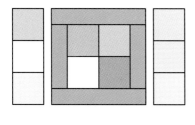

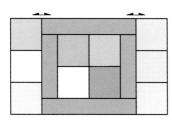

5 Select 10 assorted squares. Join them in groups of five to make two 10½"-long strips.

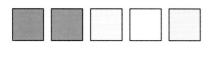

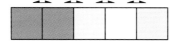

6 Sew the strips from step 5 to the unit from step 4 as shown.

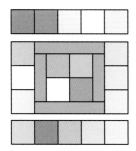 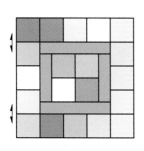

7 Sew pink 1½" × 10½" rectangles to opposite sides of the unit from step 6. Then sew pink 1½" × 12½" rectangles to the top and bottom of the unit to complete the block.

8 Repeat steps 1–7 to make a total of nine blocks with pink frames.

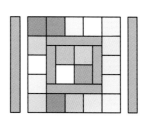 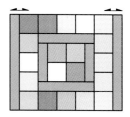

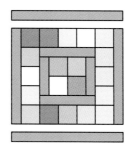 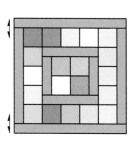

Make 9 with pink frames.

9 Repeat steps 1–7 using the off-white rectangles and assorted squares to make four blocks with off-white frames.

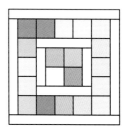

Make 4 with off-white frames.

Making the Partial Blocks

1 Lay out three assorted squares as shown. Sew two squares together, press, and then add the remaining square.

2 Sew an off-white 1½" × 5½" rectangle to the left side of the unit from step 1. Sew an off-white 1½" × 6½" rectangle to the top of the unit. The off-white strips will be longer than the unit.

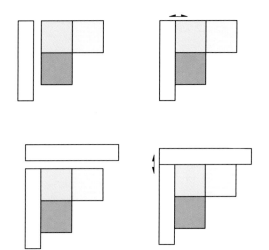

3 Select four assorted squares. Join the squares to make an 8½"-long strip.

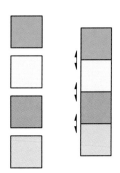

4 Sew the strip from step 3 to the left side of the unit from step 2.

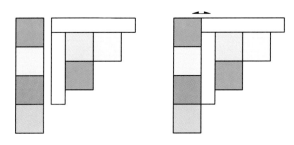

5 Select five assorted squares. Join the squares to make a 10½"-long strip.

6 Sew the strip from step 5 to the top of the unit from step 4.

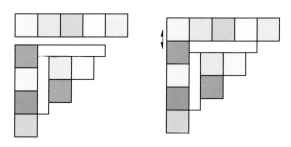

7 Sew an off-white 1½" × 11½" rectangle to the left side of the unit from step 6. Sew an off-white 1½" × 12½" rectangle to the top of the unit to complete a half block.

8 Repeat steps 1–7 to make a total of eight partial blocks.

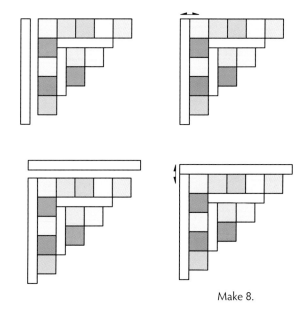

Make 8.

Making the Corner Blocks

1 Select seven assorted squares. Join five squares to make a 10½"-long pieced strip. Join two squares to make a 4½"-long pieced strip.

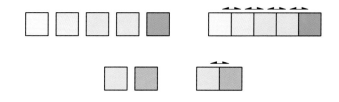

2 Arrange one off-white 1½" × 12½" rectangle, the 10½"-long pieced strip, one off-white 1½" × 6½" rectangle, and the 4½"-long pieced strip as shown. Fold each piece in half and finger-press to mark the center. Sew the pieces together, matching the center creases to make a corner block. Repeat to make a total of four corner blocks.

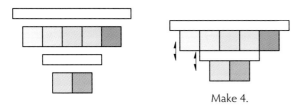

Make 4.

Assembling the Quilt Top

1 Lay out the pink blocks, off-white blocks, partial blocks, and corner blocks in diagonal rows as shown. Sew the blocks together into rows.

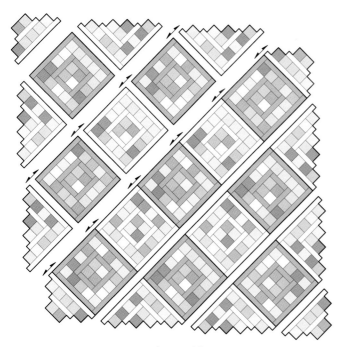

Quilt assembly

2 Sew the rows together and press. Trim and square up the quilt top, making sure to leave ¼" beyond the points of the blocks and squares for the seam allowance. Or, you can wait and trim the edges after the quilting is completed to avoid creating bias edges at this time. If you do trim prior to quilting, stay stitch around the perimeter of the quilt top, ⅛" from the edges.

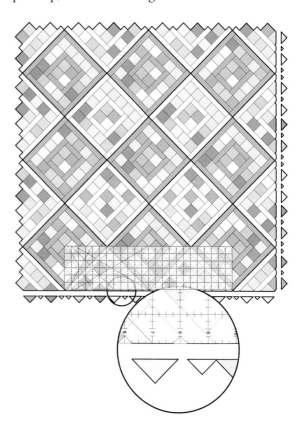

Finishing the Quilt

Go to ShopMartingale.com/HowtoQuilt if you need more information on finishing techniques.

1 Layer and baste your quilt, and quilt as desired.

2 Using the striped 2½"-wide strips, prepare and attach the binding.

Tic Tac Tile

Simple and versatile, here's a pattern that's suited to any number of fabric combinations. Depending on the fabrics you use, your version can take on a whole new look simply by choosing a bold color for the sashing.

FINISHED QUILT: 64½" × 80½" • **FINISHED BLOCK:** 8" × 8"

Designed and pieced by Rebecca Silbaugh; quilted by Steve Kooistra

Materials

Yardage is based on 42"-wide fabric.

40 precut strips, 2½" × 42", of brown solid for blocks

40 squares, 10" × 10", of assorted light or medium prints for blocks

⅔ yard of fabric for binding

5 yards of fabric for backing

72" × 88" piece of batting

Cutting

From *each* of the 40 brown solid strips, cut:

2 rectangles, 2½" × 8½" (80 total)

2 rectangles, 2½" × 4½" (80 total)

4 squares, 2½" × 2½" (160 total)

From *each* of the 40 light or medium print squares, cut:

1 strip, 4½" × 10"; crosscut into:

    1 square, 4½" × 4½" (40 total)

    2 rectangles, 2½" × 4½" (80 total)

1 rectangle, 4½" × 8½" (40 total)

From the binding fabric, cut:

8 strips, 2¼" × 42"

THEMES

To keep scrappy quilts looking cohesive rather than messy, it's best to have a theme. Using precuts makes this easy since the fabrics all came from the same line and already have a theme. But what if you're choosing your own fabrics? Consider using primarily florals, working in a limited color palette, or sticking with a particular style of fabric, such as batiks, modern prints, or Civil War reproductions. One caveat: some of the best scrappy quilts have no theme at all. Whatever route you follow, remember to relax and have fun!

Making the Blocks

Use one light (or medium) print for each block. Press the seam allowances as indicated by the arrows, or as otherwise instructed.

1 Sew brown 2½" squares to both ends of a light 2½" × 4½" rectangle. Make two units. Sew the units to both long edges of a light 4½" × 8½" rectangle. Repeat to make 40 A blocks.

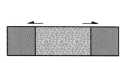 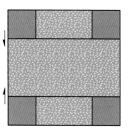

Block A.
Make 40.

2 Sew brown 2½" × 4½" rectangles to opposite sides of a light 4½" square. Sew brown 2½" × 8½" rectangles to the top and the bottom of each unit. Repeat to make 40 B blocks.

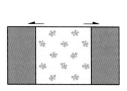 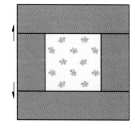

Block B.
Make 40.

Assembling the Quilt Top

1 Randomly select one A block and one B block and sew them together as shown to make a half block. Press the seam allowances toward the B block. Make 40.

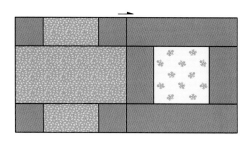

Make 40.

SUPER BLOCKS

For ease of assembly, Rebecca recommends joining the quilt blocks in groups of four to create "super blocks," as shown in step 2 below. Be sure to rotate the direction in which you press the seam allowances, as indicated by the pressing arrows, so that you have the freedom of twisting and turning the blocks as needed for color placement when laying out the quilt top. It's much easier to rotate a few larger blocks than dozens of smaller ones!

2 Sew two half blocks together to make one large block. Carefully clip the seam allowances at the intersection of the blocks; clip up to, but not through, the stitching. Press the seam allowances in a clockwise direction. Make 20 blocks.

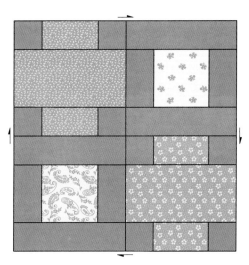

Make 20.

3 Lay out the blocks in five rows of four blocks each, orienting the blocks as shown in the quilt diagram. When you're pleased with the fabric placement, sew the blocks together into rows; press. Sew the rows together and press the seam allowances in one direction.

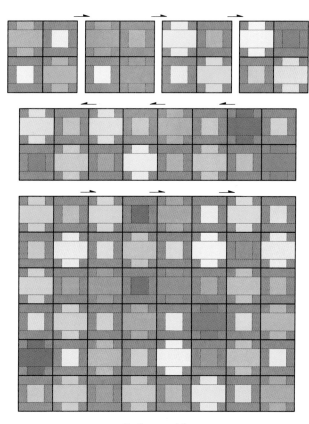

Quilt assembly

Finishing the Quilt

Go to ShopMartingale.com/HowtoQuilt if you need more information on finishing techniques.

1 Layer and baste your quilt, and quilt as desired.

2 Using the 2¼"-wide binding strips, prepare and attach the binding.

Baby Waves

This colorful rainbow of waves is sure to brighten any baby's day and bring oceans of compliments your way.

FINISHED QUILT: 48" × 60" • **FINISHED BLOCK:** 12" × 12"

Designed by Laurie Baker; pieced by Laurie Baker, Ann Unes, Margaret Ager, and Viv Browning; quilted by Sherrie Coppenbarger

Materials

Yardage is based on 42"-wide fabric.

18 precut strips, 2½" × 42", of assorted bright solids for blocks

3 yards of white solid for blocks and border

¾ yard of royal blue solid for blocks and binding

3⅓ yards of fabric for backing

54" × 66" piece of batting

SORTING YOUR STRIPS

Pick your favorite color in a darker value for the half-square-triangle units that create the pinwheels in the center of each block and at the corners where the blocks meet. Laurie chose a royal blue. Then select strips for the remaining half-square-triangle units in colors that don't compete with or overwhelm the pinwheels. This way the pinwheels stand out.

Cutting

From the 18 bright solid strips, cut a *total* of:
240 squares, 2½" × 2½"

From the white solid, cut:
18 strips, 2½" × 42"; crosscut into 288 squares, 2½" × 2½"
10 strips, 2" × 42"; crosscut into:
    96 squares, 2" × 2"
    48 rectangles, 2" × 3½"
5 strips, 6½" × 42"

From the royal blue solid, cut:
3 strips, 2½" × 42"; crosscut into 48 squares, 2½" × 2½"
6 strips, 2¼" × 42"

Making the Blocks

Press the seam allowances as indicated by the arrows, or as otherwise instructed.

1 Draw a diagonal line from corner to corner on the wrong side of each white 2½" square.

2 Place a marked white square on a royal blue 2½" square, right sides together and raw edges aligned. Stitch ¼" from both sides of the marked line. Cut the squares apart on the line, and press. Repeat with the remaining royal blue squares to make a total of 96 half-square-triangle units. Trim each unit to 2" square.

Make 96.

3 Repeat step 2 with the remaining marked white squares and the bright 2½" squares to make an additional 480 half-square-triangle units. Trim each unit to 2" square.

Make 480.

4 Arrange two blue half-square-triangle units from step 2, 10 assorted bright half-square-triangle units from step 3, two white 2" squares, and one white 2" × 3½" rectangle into four horizontal rows as shown. Be sure the blue units are positioned in the upper-left and lower-right corners. Sew the units in each row together, and then sew the rows together. Repeat to make a total of 48 units.

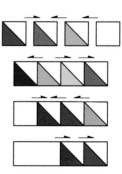 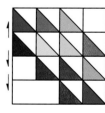

Make 48.

5 Arrange four units from step 4 into two horizontal rows of two units each, rotating the units as shown. Sew the units together into rows; press. Sew the rows together and press the seam allowances in either direction. Repeat to make a total of 12 blocks.

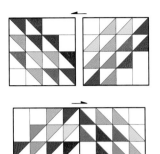 

Make 12.

Assembling the Quilt Top

1 Lay out four rows of three blocks each.

2 Sew the blocks together into rows, redirecting the seam allowances as needed so the seams oppose each other. Press the seam allowances in opposite directions from row to row. Sew the rows together and press the seam allowances in one direction.

3 Join the white 6½"-wide strips end to end. Cut four strips, 48½" long. Sew strips to the sides of the quilt top, and then sew the remaining strips to the top and bottom of the quilt top to complete the border.

Finishing the Quilt

Go to ShopMartingale.com/HowtoQuilt if you need more information on finishing techniques.

1 Layer and baste your quilt, and quilt as desired.

2 Using the royal blue 2¼"-wide strips, prepare and attach the binding.

Quilt layout

Porch Swing

///////////////

Put relaxation on your radar and stitch together the perfect cuddly quilt for enjoying a porch swing, a tall lemonade, and a good book.

FINISHED QUILT: 61½" × 61½" • **FINISHED BLOCK:** 6" × 6"

Designed and pieced by Kim Brackett; quilted by Nancy Troyer

Materials

Yardage is based on 42"-wide fabric.

13 precut strips, 2½" × 42", of assorted blue prints for blocks

6 precut strips, 2½" × 42", of assorted red prints for blocks

2⅝ yards of beige print for blocks

⅓ yard of blue print for inner border

1⅔ yards of large-scale floral for outer border and binding

4¼ yards of fabric for backing

68" × 68" piece of batting

Cutting

From the beige print, cut:

4 strips, 4½" × 42"; crosscut into 28 squares, 4½" × 4½"

26 strips, 2½" × 42"; crosscut into:

  164 rectangles, 2½" × 4½"

  72 squares, 2½" × 2½"

From *each* of the 13 blue print strips, cut:

5 rectangles, 2½" × 4½" (65 total; 1 is extra)

5 squares, 2½" × 2½" (65 total; 1 is extra)

From *each* of the 6 red print strips, cut:

12 squares, 2½" × 2½" (72 total)

From the blue print for inner border, cut:

5 strips, 1½" × 42"

From the large-scale floral, cut:

6 strips, 6" × 42"

7 strips, 2½" × 42"

CUTTING FROM YOUR STASH

Time to whittle down your fabric stash? To cut your blocks from scraps rather than using precut 2½" strips as listed in "Materials" at left, follow these instructions.

From assorted blue prints, cut:
64 rectangles, 2½" × 4½"
64 squares, 2½" × 2½"

From assorted red prints, cut:
36 pairs of squares, 2½" × 2½" (72 total)

From assorted beige prints, cut:
28 squares, 4½" × 4½"
164 rectangles, 2½" × 4½"
72 squares, 2½" × 2½"

Making the Blocks

Press the seam allowances as indicated by the arrows, or as otherwise instructed.

1 Draw a diagonal line from corner to corner on the wrong side of a blue 2½" square. Place the marked square on one end of a beige 2½" × 4½" rectangle, right sides together and corners aligned. Sew on the line. Trim the excess corner fabric, leaving a ¼" seam allowance, and press. Make 64.

Make 64.

2 Place a beige 2½" × 4½" rectangle at right angles on a blue 2½" × 4½" rectangle, right sides together and corners aligned. Draw a diagonal line on the beige rectangle as shown. Sew on the line. Trim the excess corner fabric, leaving a ¼" seam allowance, and press. Make 64.

Make 64.

3 To make block A, sew a unit from step 1 to each beige 4½" square.

Make 28.

4 Sew each unit from step 3 to a unit from step 2 as shown. Make 28 of block A.

Block A.
Make 28.

5 Referring to the technique used in step 1, make a half-square-triangle unit as shown using a beige 2½" square and a red 2½" square. Make 36 matching pairs of half-square-triangle units.

Make 36
matching pairs.

6 To make block B, sew together matching pairs of units from step 5 as shown.

Make 36.

7 Sew a beige 2½" × 4½" rectangle to each unit from step 6 as shown.

Make 36.

8 Sew a unit from step 1 to each unit from step 7 as shown.

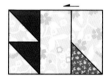

Make 36.

9 Sew a unit from step 2 to each unit from step 8. Make 36 of block B.

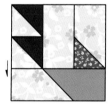

Block B.
Make 36.

Assembling the Quilt Top

1 Lay out eight horizontal rows of eight blocks each as shown, placing the A blocks around the outside edges and the B blocks in the center.

2 Sew the blocks together into rows; press. Sew the rows together and press the seam allowances in one direction.

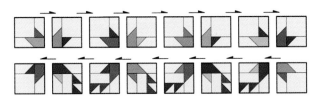

3 Join the blue 1½"-wide strips end to end. Measure the length of the quilt top through the center. Cut two strips to that measurement and sew them to the sides of the quilt top. Press the seam allowances away from the center. Measure the width of the quilt top through the center, including the borders just added. Cut two strips to that measurement and sew them to the top and bottom of the quilt top to complete the inner border. Press the seam allowances away from the center.

4 Repeat with the floral 6"-wide strips to add the outer border.

Finishing the Quilt

Go to ShopMartingale.com/HowtoQuilt if you need more information on finishing techniques.

1 Layer and baste your quilt, and quilt as desired.

2 Using the floral 2½"-wide strips, prepare and attach the binding.

Ladybugs!

Simple patchwork, easy appliqué shapes, and chain-stitch embroidery details bring this quilt to life. These darling appliqué motifs work well with any group of fabrics and will happily adorn either yardage or 5" charm squares.

FINISHED QUILT: 62½" × 70½" • **FINISHED BLOCK:** 8" × 8"

Designed by Adrienne Smitke; pieced by Adrienne Smitke and Cathy Valentine Reitan; machine appliquéd by Karen Costello Soltys; machine quilted by Karen Burns

Materials

Yardage is based on 42"-wide fabric.

11 or more strips, 2½" × 21", of assorted medium to dark prints for pieced blocks

11 strips, 2½" × 42", of assorted light prints for pieced blocks

1⅝ yards of cream fabric for appliqué background

¼ yard *each* of pink polka dot and red polka dot for ladybug appliqués

¼ yard *each* of pink, teal, and blue prints for flower appliqués

⅛ yard of brown solid for ladybug details

Assorted scraps (or strip leftovers) for leaf and flower-center appliqués

½ yard of teal leaf print for inner border

2 yards of red print for outer border and binding

4 yards of fabric for backing

69" × 77" piece of batting

Template plastic

1¼ yards of 18"-wide fusible web (optional)

Brown embroidery floss

Sorting Your Strips

For each patchwork block, you'll need two contrasting medium or dark fabric strips and one light strip. Each set of fabrics will yield enough pieces for two blocks. If you want a scrappier quilt, you can select a different set of strips for each block and you'll have leftovers for another project.

Cutting

For *each* of 21 blocks, cut:
    From 2 medium to dark 2½" × 42" strips:
        4 squares, 2½" × 2½" (8 total)
    From a light 2½" × 42" strip:
        4 rectangles, 2½" × 4½"

From the cream fabric, cut:
21 squares, 8½" × 8½"

From the teal leaf print, cut:
6 strips, 1½" × 42"

From the red print, cut:
7 strips, 6½" × 42"
7 strips, 2½" × 42"

Making the Pieced Blocks

For each block, select four matching print 2½" squares, four matching but contrasting print 2½" squares, and four matching light 2½" × 4½" rectangles. Press the seam allowances as indicated by the arrows, or as otherwise instructed.

1 Sew two print and two contrasting print squares together as shown to make a four-patch unit.

2 Sew a print square to one end of a light 2½" × 4½" rectangle. Sew a contrasting print square to the other end as shown. Make two matching units.

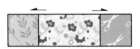

Make 2.

3 Sew light 2½" × 4½" rectangles to opposite sides of the four-patch unit from step 1. Then sew the units from step 2 to the top and bottom of the block as shown. Make sure the colors are positioned so that each forms a diagonal line of like-colored squares. Press. Repeat to make a total of 21 blocks.

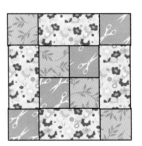

Make 21.

Making the Appliquéd Blocks

1 Using the patterns on pages 83–85 and the fabric suggestions in "Materials" on page 79, prepare five of flower A, five of flower B, four of flower C, and eight ladybugs for your preferred method of appliqué. In the quilt shown, Karen Soltys used fusible-web appliqué with machine stitching; for details on appliqué techniques, visit ShopMartingale.com/HowtoQuilt. (The patterns provided have been reversed and, for fusible appliqué, you should not add seam allowances.)

EFFICIENT USE OF FUSIBLE WEB

If fusible-web appliqué is your method of choice, you can save on the amount of fusible product you use by tracing smaller detail shapes inside of larger ones. For example, rather than cover the ladybug's entire body with fusible web, which will just make her stiff and inflexible, trace the outline of the large circle onto the fusible web. Then trace the two small circles and the wedge-shaped head inside of the large circle.

Cut out the small circles and the wedge, leaving about ¼" outside of each shape. Then cut away any odd bits of fusible web remaining, leaving just ¼" of web inside the marked outer circle. That gives you enough web to adhere the ladybug to the quilt block and the blanket stitching will secure it in place. The body of the ladybug will remain soft and flexible, just as if it had been hand appliquéd. You can use this same trick for the flowers and flower centers.

Trace detail pieces inside larger ones.

Cut shapes, leaving ¼" inside and outside of marked line.

2 Referring to the placement guides on the patterns, position the flowers, flower centers, and leaves onto the cream 8½" squares and appliqué in place. In the same manner, add the ladybugs and brown details. You will have one ladybug left over; she is attached to the corner of the quilt top once it's been assembled.

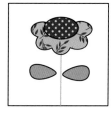
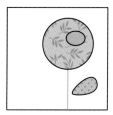

3 If desired, machine blanket stitch or satin stitch around each shape to secure the edges and add textural details. To help define the shapes in the quilt shown, brown machine-quilting thread was used for the machine stitching. See the tip box on page 81 for more details on doing blanket stitch by machine.

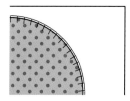

4 Using two strands of brown embroidery floss and a stem stitch, embroider the flower stems, ladybug antennae, and dark lines on the back of the ladybugs to indicate wing separation.

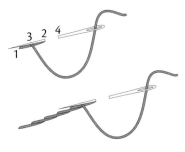
Stem stitch

MACHINE BLANKET STITCH

If you love doing handwork, you may want to blanket stitch around each appliqué shape by hand with brown embroidery floss. However, you can make quick work of this if your sewing machine has a built-in blanket stitch feature. Here are some tips for stitching by machine.

Adjust the tension before beginning. Karen used machine quilting thread in the needle and regular sewing thread in the bobbin. Loosen the tension so that the bobbin thread doesn't pull up to the top of the block as you stitch. Test a sample and readjust as needed until you're happy with the results. If necessary, use a tear-away stabilizer under the block to help the machine stitch more smoothly.

The blanket stitch is a two-part stitch. One part of the stitch moves forward, along the edge of the appliqué. The other part "bites" into the appliqué and back to the edge. Position the appliqué under the needle so that the forward stitch is just off the edge of the appliqué and stitching into the background fabric only. The other portion of the stitch should bite into the appliqué fabric perpendicular to the edge of the fabric.

Stitch slowly and raise the presser foot after every few stitches to turn the fabric so that the stitches flow smoothly around each shape. Don't turn the fabric while the needle is taking a bite into the

appliqué shape, but instead, turn it while the needle is on the outside of the shape. This way, you won't create a visible V in the stitch.

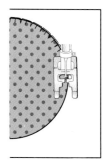

Rotate with needle in background fabric.   Don't rotate with needle in appliqué fabric.

To secure the threads, as you near the end of the stitching, pull the top starting thread so that it aligns with the edge of the appliqué. That way you can stitch over it without it showing and the beginning stitches will be secured. To knot the end of the thread, raise the needle, switch the stitch back to the straight stitch, set the stitch length to zero, and stitch two or three times in place. Clip all threads close to the surface. Remove the stabilizer if you used one, but tear away carefully to prevent distorting the stitches.

Assembling the Quilt Top

1. Lay out seven rows of six blocks each, alternating the appliqué blocks with the pieced blocks. Play with the arrangement until you are satisfied with the color placement. Ladybugs can rotate any which way, but you may want all flower stems to face in the same direction.

2. Sew the blocks together into rows; press. Sew the rows together and press the seam allowances in one direction.

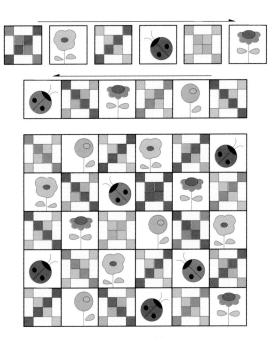

Quilt assembly

3. Join the teal 1½"-wide strips end to end. Measure the length of the quilt top through the center. Cut two strips to that measurement and sew them to the sides of the quilt top. Press the seam allowances away from the center. Measure the width of the quilt top through the center, including the borders just added. Cut two strips to that measurement and sew them to the top and bottom of the quilt top to complete the inner border. Press.

4. Repeat with the red 6½"-wide strips to add the outer border.

5. Once the quilt top is complete, appliqué the final ladybug to the bottom-right corner, as shown in the diagram below. Don't forget to add the blanket-stitch and stem-stitch details.

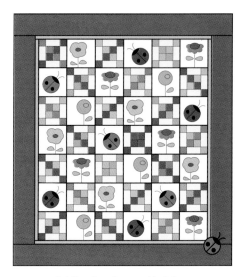

Adding borders and ladybug

Finishing the Quilt

Go to ShopMartingale.com/HowtoQuilt if you need more information on finishing techniques.

1. Layer and baste your quilt, and quilt as desired.

2. Using the red 2½"-wide strips, prepare and attach the binding.

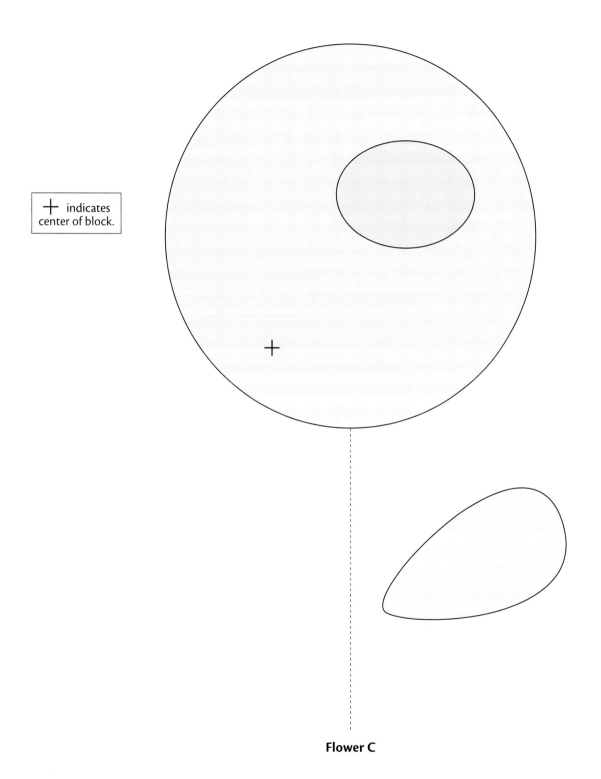

+ indicates
center of block.

Flower C

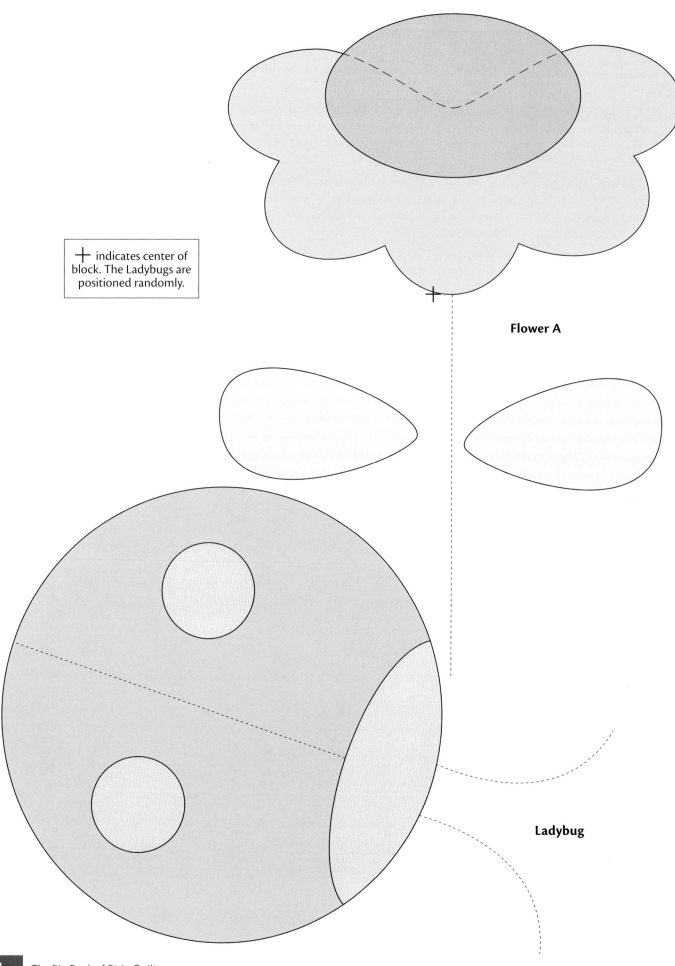

+ indicates center of
block. The Ladybugs are
positioned randomly.

Flower A

Ladybug

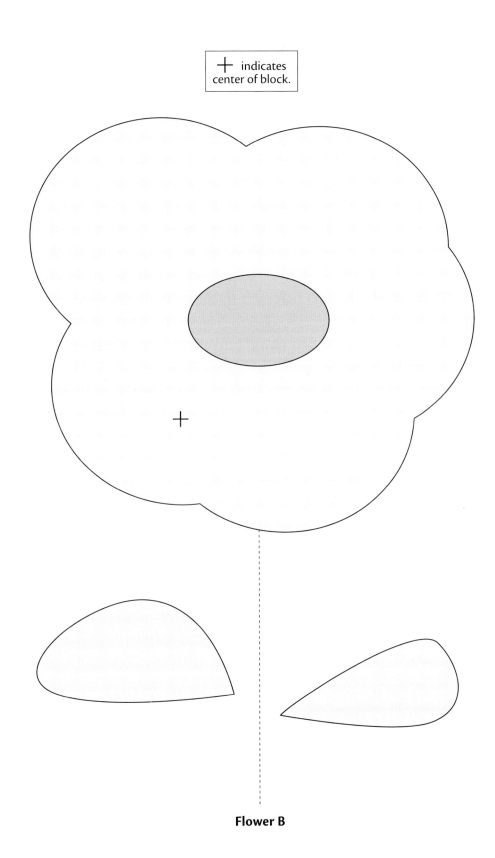

+ indicates center of block.

Flower B

Buttoned Up

The precise placement of fabric and buttons gives this quilt its buttoned-up look. There are angles aplenty, but you can soften them by using an array of your most congenial prints.

FINISHED QUILT: 62½" × 62½" • **FINISHED BLOCK:** 8" × 8"

Designed and pieced by Gerri Robinson; machine quilted by Rebecca Segura

Materials

Yardage is based on 42"-wide fabric.

36 precut strips, 2½" × 42", of assorted bright prints for blocks

3 yards of white solid for block backgrounds and inner border

2 yards of teal print for outer border

⅝ yard of orange print for binding

4¼ yards of fabric for backing

70" × 70" piece of batting

36 orange buttons, ⅞" diameter

Cutting

From *each* of the 36 bright print strips, cut:

8 rectangles, 2½" × 4½" (288 total)

From the white solid, cut:

36 strips, 2½" × 42"; crosscut into 576 squares, 2½" × 2½"

5 strips, 1½" × 42"

From the teal print, cut on the *lengthwise* grain:

2 strips, 6½" × 54"

2 strips, 6½" × 66"

From the orange print, cut:

7 strips, 2½" × 42"

Making the Blocks

Press the seam allowances as indicated by the arrows, or as otherwise instructed.

1 Draw a diagonal line from corner to corner on the wrong side of two white 2½" squares. Place a marked square on one end of a bright 2½" × 4½" rectangle, right sides together and corners aligned. Sew on the line. Trim the excess corner fabric, leaving a ¼" seam allowance, and press. Sew the second white square to the other end of the rectangle, being careful to position the seam as shown. Make a total of 36 sets of eight matching units (288 total).

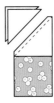

Make 288.

2 Sew two matching units from step 1 together as shown to make a 4½" square. Make a total of 144 units.

Make 144.

3 Sew four matching units from step 2 together, rotating them as shown, to make a block. The block should measure 8½" square. Make a total of 36 blocks.

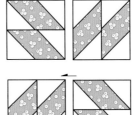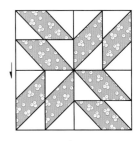

Make 36.

Assembling the Quilt Top

1 Lay out the blocks in six rows of six blocks each, as shown below.

2 Sew the blocks together into rows; press. Sew the rows together and press the seam allowances in one direction. The quilt center should measure 48½" square.

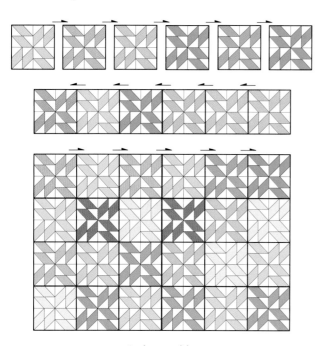

Quilt assembly

3 Join the white 1½"-wide strips end to end. Measure the length of the quilt top through the center. Cut two strips to that measurement and sew them to the sides of the quilt top. Measure the width of the quilt top through the center, including the side borders just added. Cut two strips to that measurement and sew them to the top and bottom of the quilt top to complete the inner border.

4 Sew the teal 6½" × 54" strips to the sides of the quilt top, and then sew the teal 6½" × 66" strips to the top and bottom of the quilt top to complete the outer border.

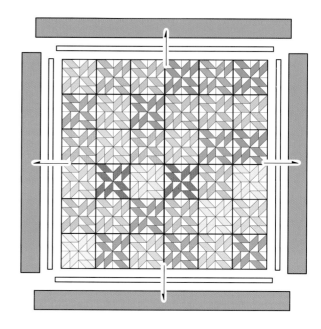

Finishing the Quilt

Go to ShopMartingale.com/HowtoQuilt if you need more information on finishing techniques.

1 Layer and baste your quilt, and quilt as desired.

2 Using the orange 2½"-wide strips, prepare and attach the binding.

3 Sew an orange button in the center of each block.

Rose Garden

In tribute to the lovely Rose City (Portland, Oregon), where she was born, Adrienne Smitke created a quilted interpretation of beautifully manicured rows of flowers. Warm pinks, golds, and reds appear to bloom under a summer sun, but you can vary the colors to cultivate your own perfect rose garden.

FINISHED QUILT: 83½" × 83½" • **FINISHED BLOCK:** 10½" × 10½"

Designed and pieced by Adrienne Smitke; machine quilted by Karen Burns

Materials

Yardage is based on 42"-wide fabric.

36 precut strips, 2½" × 42", of assorted prints
   for blocks

36 squares, 5" × 5", of assorted prints for blocks

2¼ yards of cream solid for block backgrounds

⅞ yard of green print for blocks

⅞ yard of pale yellow print for blocks and inner
   border

2⅞ yards of red print for outer border and binding

7½ yards of fabric for backing

90" × 90" piece of batting

Cutting

From *each* of the 36 print strips, cut:

2 rectangles, 2½" × 5" (72 total)

2 rectangles, 2½" × 9" (72 total)

From the cream solid, cut:

29 strips, 2½" × 42"; crosscut into:

   216 squares, 2½" × 2½"

   72 rectangles, 2½" × 7"

From the green print, cut:

9 strips, 2½" × 42"; crosscut into 144 squares,
   2½" × 2½"

From the pale yellow print, cut:

10 strips, 2½" × 42"; crosscut *3 strips* into 36 squares,
   2½" × 2½"

From the red print, cut:

8 strips, 8½" × 42"

9 strips, 2½" × 42"

Making the Blocks

Press the seam allowances as indicated by the arrows,
or as otherwise instructed.

1. Draw a diagonal line from corner to corner on
   the wrong side of two cream 2½" squares. Place
   a marked square on each end of a print 2½" × 9"
   rectangle as shown above right, right sides
   together and corners aligned. Sew on the lines.

Trim, leaving ¼" seam allowances, and press.
Make two each of 36 matching colors, 72 total.

Make 2 each of 36 matching colors.

2. Sew two matching 2½" × 5" rectangles and two
   matching units from step 1 to a print 5" square.
   Make 36 flower units.

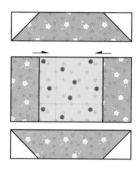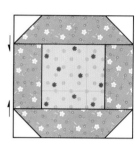

Make 36.

3. Referring to the technique used in step 1, make a
   half-square-triangle unit as shown using a cream
   2½" square and a green 2½" square. Make 72.

Make 72.

4. Referring again to step 1, place a marked green
   2½" square on one end of a cream 2½" × 7"
   rectangle. Stitch, trim, and press. Make 36 with
   the seam angle going in one direction and 36
   with the angle going in the opposite direction.

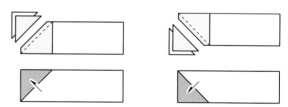

Make 36 of each.

5 Join 36 of the units from step 3 and 36 of the units from step 4 to make the side leaf units.

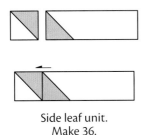

Side leaf unit.
Make 36.

6 Join the remaining units from steps 3 and 4 with the pale yellow 2½" squares to make the top leaf units. Make 36.

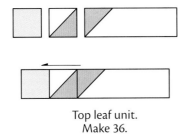

Top leaf unit.
Make 36.

7 Attach a side leaf unit and a top leaf unit to each flower unit. Make 36.

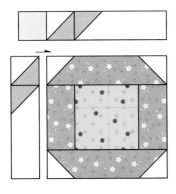

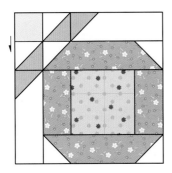

Make 36.

Assembling the Quilt Top

1 Arrange the blocks in groups of four, rotating them so that the leaf units are in the outer corners and the flower units meet at the center. Don't sew the blocks together yet. Lay out three rows of three groups each as shown.

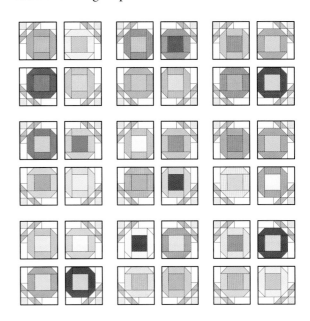

2 Once you're happy with the placement of the fabrics, sew the groups of four blocks together, making sure to match the seams at the block centers. Sew the groups together into rows; press. Sew the rows together and press the seam allowances in one direction.

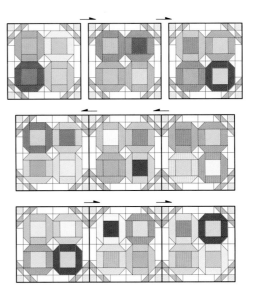

3 Join the pale yellow 2½"-wide strips end to end. Measure the length of the quilt top through the center. Cut two strips to that measurement and sew them to the sides of the quilt top. Measure the width of the quilt top through the center, including the borders just added. Cut two strips to that measurement and sew them to the top and bottom of the quilt top to complete the inner border.

4 Repeat with the red 8½"-wide strips to add the outer border.

Finishing the Quilt

Go to ShopMartingale.com/HowtoQuilt if you need more information on finishing techniques.

1 Layer and baste your quilt, and quilt as desired.

2 Using the red 2½"-wide strips, prepare and attach the binding.

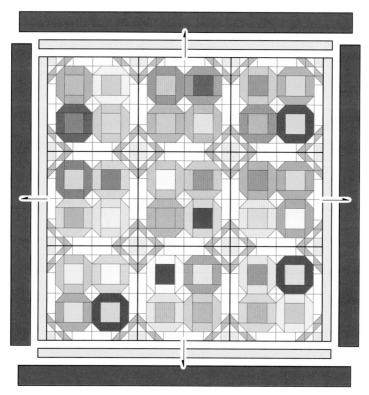

Quilt assembly

Modern Mirrors

////////////

This striking quilt is big, beautiful, and simple. It could easily be scaled down to suit your desired size—but once you start picking out strips to use, you might not want to stop!

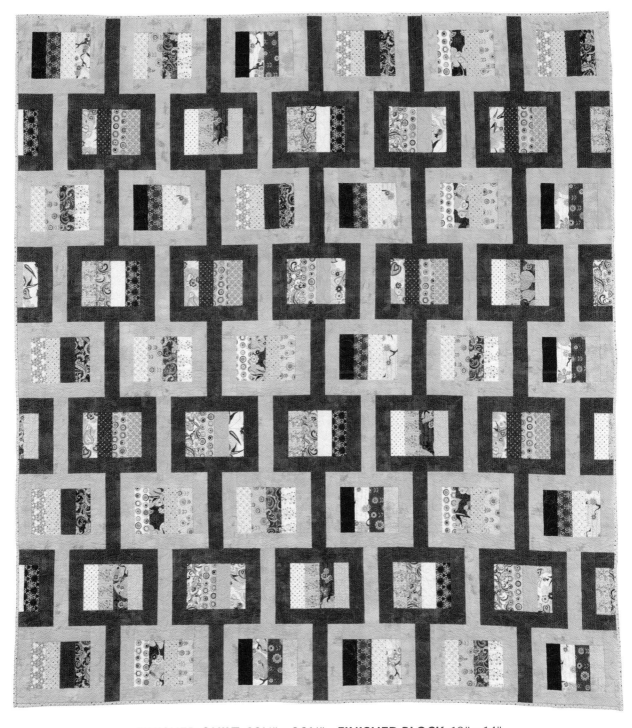

FINISHED QUILT: 82½" × 90½" • **FINISHED BLOCK:** 10" × 14"

Designed and pieced by Amy Ellis; machine quilted by Natalia Bonner

Materials

Yardage is based on 42"-wide fabric.

36 precut strips, 2½" × 42", of assorted prints for blocks*

3¼ yards of aqua print for blocks

3 yards of brown solid for blocks

¾ yard of pink print for binding

6¾ yards of fabric for backing

91" × 99" piece of batting

Or 2⅞ yards total of assorted prints cut into 36 strips, 2½" × 42"

Cutting

From the aqua print, cut:

36 strips, 2½" × 42"; crosscut *18 strips* into:
  60 rectangles, 2½" × 8½"
  30 rectangles, 2½" × 10½"

From the brown solid, cut:

30 strips, 2½" × 42"; crosscut *12 strips* into:
  48 rectangles, 2½" × 8½"
  24 rectangles, 2½" × 10½"

From the pink print, cut:

9 strips, 2½" × 42"

Making the Blocks

Press the seam allowances as indicated by the arrows, or as otherwise instructed.

1. Sew together four assorted 2½" × 42" strips to make a strip set. Make nine strip sets.

Make 9 strip sets.

2. Cut the strip sets into 54 center segments, 6½" wide.

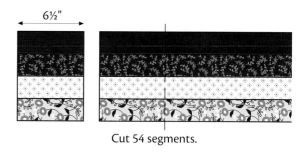

6½"

Cut 54 segments.

3. Sew an aqua 2½" × 8½" rectangle to a center segment as shown. Sew a brown 2½" × 8½" rectangle to a center segment as shown. Make 30 aqua units and 24 brown units.

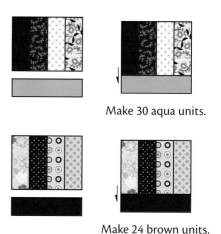

Make 30 aqua units.

Make 24 brown units.

4. Sew an aqua 2½" × 8½" rectangle to the left side of an aqua unit, and sew a brown 2½" × 8½" rectangle to the left side of a brown unit. Make 30 aqua units and 24 brown units.

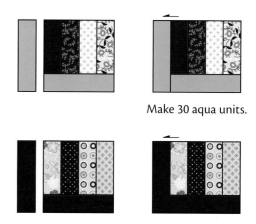

Make 30 aqua units.

Make 24 brown units.

5 Sew an aqua 2½" × 10½" rectangle to the top of an aqua unit, and sew a brown 2½" × 10½" rectangle to the top of a brown unit. Make 30 aqua units and 24 brown units.

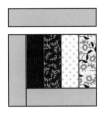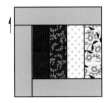

Make 30 aqua units.

Make 24 brown units.

6 Sew an aqua 2½" × 42" strip to a brown 2½" × 42" strip to make a strip set. Make 18 strip sets.

Make 18 strip sets.

7 Cut the strip sets from step 6 into 54 segments, 10½" wide.

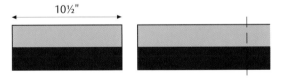

10½"

Cut 54 segments.

8 Pin and sew the 10½" segments from step 7 to the right side of the units from step 5, placing the appropriate-colored strip next to the block to match the aqua or brown unit. Make 30 aqua blocks and 24 brown blocks. Trim the blocks to 10½" × 14½".

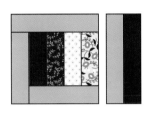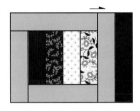

Make 30 aqua blocks.

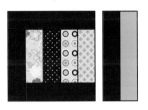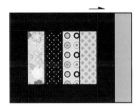

Make 24 brown blocks.

Assembling the Quilt Top

This top is a little challenging to put together, but the result is worth it! Make sure you have plenty of work space for laying out your blocks.

1 Lay out six aqua blocks in a row. Pin and sew the blocks together. Press the seam allowances toward the right. Undo the stitching and remove the last brown strip at the right end of the row. The row should measure 82½". Make five aqua rows.

Remove last brown strip.

Make 5 aqua rows.

2 Cut four brown blocks between the second and third of the four print strips as shown; the right piece is one strip wider than the left piece.

3 Lay out the brown row as shown, with the half blocks placed on either end. Pin and sew the blocks together. Press the seam allowances toward the left. Evenly trim the ends of the row to measure 82½". This compensates for the brown strip that was removed in step 1. Repeat to make four brown rows.

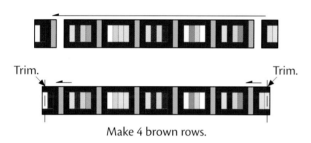

Trim.   Trim.

Make 4 brown rows.

4 Lay out the aqua and brown rows in alternating positions, keeping the directions of the pressed seam allowances as shown. Sew the rows together and press the seam allowances in one direction.

Finishing the Quilt

Go to ShopMartingale.com/HowtoQuilt if you need more information on finishing techniques.

1 Layer and baste your quilt, and quilt as desired.

2 Using the pink 2½"-wide strips, prepare and attach the binding.

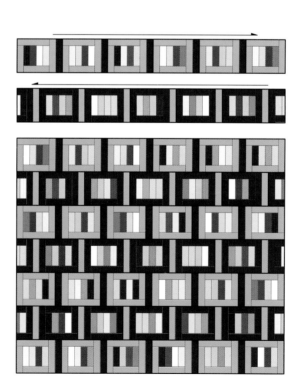

Journeys

Uncluttered and contemporary, this versatile design works well with different fabric styles and colorways. Does the path lead out or in? Does it matter? After all, the joy is in the journey, not the destination!

FINISHED QUILT: 68½" × 84½" • **FINISHED BLOCK:** 14" × 18"

Designed and pieced by Susan Guzman; machine quilted by Linda Barrett

Materials

Yardage is based on 42"-wide fabric.

2⅝ yards of gray print for blocks, sashing, and border

1⅜ yards of navy print for blocks*

1⅝ yards of ivory print for blocks*

2 yards of blue print for blocks, sashing, border, and binding

5½ yards of fabric for backing

77" × 93" piece of batting

Susan used utility linen in place of 100% cotton for these fabrics.

Cutting

Block pieces have been lettered to help keep them organized during the assembly process.

From the gray print, cut:

33 strips, 2½" × 42"; crosscut into:

    24 rectangles, 2½" × 4½" (A)
    24 rectangles, 2½" × 8½" (B)
    24 rectangles, 2½" × 12½" (C)
    4 rectangles, 2½" × 14½" (E)
    4 rectangles, 2½" × 16½" (D)
    4 strips, 2½" × 32½" (F)
    2 strips, 2½" × 34½" (G)
    4 strips, 2½" × 36½" (H)
    2 strips, 2½" × 40½" (I)

From the navy print, cut:

16 strips, 2½" × 42"; crosscut into:

    16 rectangles, 2½" × 4½" (A)
    16 rectangles, 2½" × 8½" (B)
    16 rectangles, 2½" × 12½" (C)
    4 rectangles, 2½" × 14½" (E)
    4 rectangles, 2½" × 16½" (D)

From the ivory print, cut:

20 strips, 2½" × 42"; crosscut into:

    16 rectangles, 2½" × 4½" (A)
    16 rectangles, 2½" × 8½" (B)
    16 rectangles, 2½" × 12½" (C)
    8 rectangles, 2½" × 14½" (E)
    8 rectangles, 2½" × 16½" (D)

From the blue print, cut:

18 strips, 2½" × 42"; crosscut into:

    8 rectangles, 2½" × 4½" (A)
    8 rectangles, 2½" × 8½" (B)
    8 rectangles, 2½" × 12½" (C)
    4 strips, 2½" × 32½" (F)
    2 strips, 2½" × 34½" (G)
    4 strips, 2½" × 36½" (H)
    2 strips, 2½" × 40½" (I)

8 strips, 2¼" × 42"

Making the Blocks

Press the seam allowances as indicated by the arrows, or as otherwise instructed.

1. Sew a gray A rectangle to the long side of a navy A rectangle. Sew a navy A rectangle to the top of the unit and a gray A rectangle to the bottom of the unit as shown. Make a total of four units.

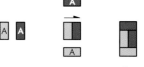

Make 4.

2. Sew a gray B rectangle to the right side of a unit from step 1 and a navy B rectangle to the left side of the unit as shown. Then sew gray and navy B rectangles to the top and bottom of the unit as shown. Make a total of four units.

Make 4.

3 Sew a navy C rectangle to the right side of a unit from step 2 and a gray C rectangle to the left side of the unit as shown. Then sew navy and gray C rectangles to the top and bottom of the unit as shown. Make a total of four units.

Make 4.

4 Sew a gray D rectangle to the right side of the unit. Sew a gray E rectangle to the top of the unit to complete the block. Make a total of four of block 1.

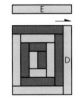

Block 1.
Make 4.

5 Repeat steps 1–4 to make a total of four of block 3, making sure to reverse the positions of the gray and navy rectangles.

Block 3.
Make 4.

6 Repeat steps 1–3 using the ivory A, B, and C rectangles and the blue A, B, and C rectangles to make four units. Then sew an ivory D rectangle to the left side of each unit and an ivory E rectangle to the top of each unit to make four of block 2.

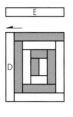

Block 2.
Make 4.

7 Repeat steps 1–3 using the remaining ivory A, B, and C rectangles and the remaining gray A, B, and C rectangles to make four units. Then sew an ivory D rectangle to the left side of each unit and an ivory E rectangle to the top of each unit to make four of block 4.

Block 4.
Make 4.

Assembling the Quilt Top

1 Lay out two of block 1 and two of block 2 in two rows, making sure to rotate the blocks in the bottom row. Sew the blocks together into rows. Join the rows to complete the section. Make two sections.

2 Sew the blue H strips to opposite sides of each
section from step 1. Then sew the blue F strips to
the top and bottom of the section. Add a gray I
strip to the left side and a gray G strip to the top
of the section. Repeat to make a second identical
section.

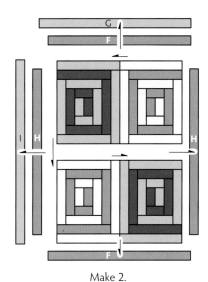

Make 2.

3 Repeat steps 1 and 2 using blocks 3 and 4, the
gray F and H strips, and the blue G and I strips to
make two sections as shown.

Make 2.

4 Lay out the sections in two rows of two as shown
in the quilt diagram. Sew the sections together
into rows, and then sew the rows together.

Quilt assembly

Finishing the Quilt

Go to ShopMartingale.com/HowtoQuilt if you need
more information on finishing techniques.

1 Layer and baste your quilt, and quilt as desired.

2 Using the blue 2¼"-wide strips, prepare and
attach binding.

Island Chain

////////////

Pick a variety of medium to dark batiks to keep the chain design sharp and clear. Carefully choosing and placing fabrics that contrast well with their neighbors will allow the "links" to appear as if they're woven together.

FINISHED QUILT: 53½" × 64¾" • **FINISHED BLOCK:** 4" × 4"

Designed, pieced, and quilted by Kim Brackett

Materials

Yardage is based on 42"-wide fabric.

40 strips, at least 2½" × 30", of assorted medium to dark batiks for blocks

1⅓ yards of light batik for blocks and setting triangles

⅞ yard of brown batik for border

⅝ yard of multicolored batik for binding

3¾ yards of fabric for backing

57½" × 68¾" piece of batting

Arranging the Strips

Before you begin cutting, lay out the 40 strips of medium to dark batik side by side, making sure that each fabric contrasts with the fabric next to it. Assign a placement order to the 40 fabrics using the block layout diagram on page 103 as a guide. You may find it helpful to label each strip with a numbered sticky note. As you cut the strips, keep the pieces together and in their placement order or numbered.

Cutting

From *each* of the 40 medium to dark batik strips, cut:

4 rectangles, 2½" × 4½" (160 total)

2 squares, 2½" × 2½" (80 total)

From the light batik, cut:

2 strips, 6⅞" × 42"; crosscut into 9 squares, 6⅞" × 6⅞". Cut the squares into quarters diagonally to yield 36 triangles.

3 strips, 4½" × 42"; crosscut into 22 squares, 4½" × 4½"

6 strips, 2½" × 42"; crosscut into 80 squares, 2½" × 2½"

From the brown batik, cut:

6 strips, 4½" × 42"

From the multicolored batik, cut:

7 strips, 2½" × 42"

//

CUTTING FROM YOUR STASH

Time to whittle down your fabric stash? To cut your blocks from scraps rather than using precut 2½" strips as listed in "Materials" at left, follow these instructions.

From assorted dark prints, cut:

40 sets of:

    4 rectangles, 2½" × 4½" (160 total)

    2 squares, 2½" × 2½" (80 total)

From assorted light prints, cut:

9 squares, 6⅞" × 6⅞"; cut the squares into quarters diagonally to yield 36 triangles

22 squares, 4½" × 4½"

80 squares, 2½" × 2½"

Making the Blocks

Press the seam allowances as indicated by the arrows, or as otherwise instructed.

1. Sew a medium to dark batik 2½" square to a light batik 2½" square. Make two units from each of the 40 medium to dark batiks.

Make 2 from each fabric.

2. Sew a matching medium to dark batik 2½" × 4½" rectangle to the top of each unit from step 1.

Make 2 from each fabric.

3. Sew together the remaining medium to dark batik 2½" × 4½" rectangles in pairs as follows: fabric 1 to fabric 2; fabric 2 to fabric 3; fabric 3 to fabric 4. Continue pairing up the rectangles

in this manner through fabric 27. *Sew fabric 28 to fabric 1;* then sew fabric 29 to 30; fabric 30 to 31; fabric 31 to 32. Continue pairing up the rectangles in this manner through fabric 39. *Sew fabric 40 to fabric 29.* Press. Stack the rectangle units in the order sewn for ease in laying out your blocks.

Assembling the Quilt Top

1 Arrange the blocks from step 2 of "Making the Blocks," the light batik 4½" squares, and the light batik setting triangles as shown.

Block layout

2 Refer to the quilt assembly diagram at right to fill in the open areas with the corresponding rectangle units from step 3 of "Making the Blocks."

3 Sew the blocks together in diagonal rows. Press the seam allowances open. Sew the rows together, adding the upper-left and lower-right corners last. Press the seam allowances open.

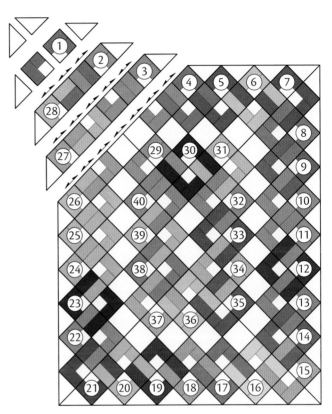

Quilt assembly

4 Join the brown batik 4½"-wide strips end to end. Measure the length of the quilt top through the center. Cut two strips to this measurement and sew them to the sides of the quilt top. Press the seam allowances toward the borders. Measure the width of the quilt top through the center, including the borders just added. Cut two strips to this measurement and sew them to the top and bottom of the quilt top to complete the border. Press the seam allowances open.

Finishing the Quilt

Go to ShopMartingale.com/HowtoQuilt if you need more information on finishing techniques.

1 Layer and baste your quilt, and quilt as desired.

2 Using the multicolored batik 2½"-wide strips, prepare and attach the binding.

Chutes and Ladders

Reminiscent of the classic board game Chutes and Ladders, cheery lines of color meander up, down, and all around. The sewing in this project is very easy with just squares and rectangles, but the setting is a little tricky, so be on your toes!

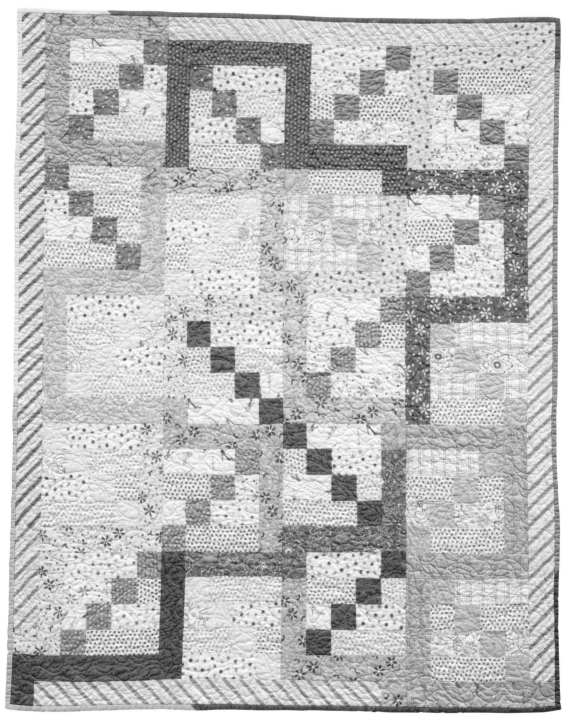

FINISHED QUILT: 44" × 54" • **FINISHED BLOCK:** 8" × 8"

Designed and pieced by Mary J. Burns; machine quilted by Karen Burns of Compulsive Quilting

Materials

Yardage is based on 42"-wide fabric.

16 precut strips, 2½" × 42", of assorted cream prints for blocks*

6 or 7 precut strips, 2½" × 42", of assorted blue prints for blocks, sashing, and border

5 precut strips, 2½" × 42", of assorted green prints for blocks, sashing, and border

3 or 4 precut strips, 2½" × 42", of assorted yellow prints for blocks, sashing, and border

3 precut strips, 2½" × 42", of assorted orange prints for blocks, sashing, and border

5 or 6 precut strips, 2½" × 42", of assorted red prints for sashing and border

5 precut strips, 2½" × 42", of assorted prints for scrappy binding*

3 yards of fabric for backing

50" × 60" piece of batting

Or 1¼ yards total of assorted cream prints cut into 16 strips, 2½" × 42"

Cutting

For Ladder Blocks

From 2 different orange strips, cut a *total* of:
24 squares, 2½" × 2½"

From 2 different blue strips, cut a *total* of:
24 squares, 2½" × 2½"

From 1 green strip, cut:
16 squares, 2½" × 2½"

From 1 yellow strip, cut:
16 squares, 2½" × 2½"

From the 16 assorted cream strips, cut a *total* of:
40 rectangles, 2½" × 6½"
40 rectangles, 2½" × 4½"
40 squares, 2½" × 2½"

For Sashing (Chutes) and Borders

If you want to control the placement of each fabric, refer to the quilt layout diagram on page 107 before cutting.

From 1 red strip, cut:*
1 strip, 2½" × 38½"
1 square, 2½" × 2½"

From the assorted red strips, cut:
7 strips, 2½" × 10½"
5 strips, 2½" × 8½"
1 strip, 2½" × 6½"
4 squares, 2½" × 2½"

From 1 blue strip, cut:
1 strip, 2½" × 28½"
1 strip, 2½" × 8½"

From the assorted blue strips, cut:
7 strips, 2½" × 10½"
5 strips, 2½" × 8½"
4 squares, 2½" × 2½"

From 1 green strip, cut:*
1 strip, 2½" × 28½"
1 strip, 2½" × 12½"

From the assorted green strips, cut:
4 strips, 2½" × 10½"
2 strips, 2½" × 8½"
2 strips, 2½" × 6½"
2 squares, 2½" × 2½"

From the assorted yellow strips, cut:
2 strips, 2½" × 10½"
6 strips, 2½" × 8½"
1 strip, 2½" × 6½"
1 strip, 2½" × 4½"
1 square, 2½" × 2½"

From 1 orange strip, cut:
1 strip, 2½" × 38½"

Mary's fabrics had over 41" of usable width after the selvages were trimmed. If your fabric has less usable width you'll need to cut the smaller pieces from a different print.

Making the Blocks

The blocks in this quilt are labeled A and B; they're made with the same sizes and quantities of pieces, but the direction of the diagonal line of squares varies between the blocks. Pay close attention to the placement as you sew so that your chutes-and-ladders arrangement will work out in the final setting. Press the seam allowances as indicated by the arrows, or as otherwise instructed.

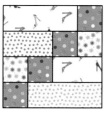 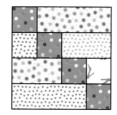

A block   B block

Block A

For each block you'll need four matching colored 2½" squares and two each of the following assorted cream pieces: 2½" × 6½", 2½" × 4½", and 2½" × 2½".

1. Sew a colored square to one end of a cream 2½" × 6½" strip. Make two.

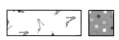 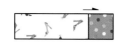

Make 2.

2. Sew a colored square between a cream 2½" × 4½" strip and a cream 2½" square. Make two.

  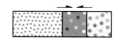

Make 2.

RAINY-DAY FUN

Play Chutes and Ladders on your quilt! Use small beanie animals as markers, starting in the top-left corner. Roll dice to move the animals back and forth on the quilt's chutes and ladders. Make up your own rules and have fun!

3. Rotate the pieces as shown and sew them together in four rows to make an A block. Repeat to make a total of 10 blocks: 2 orange, 5 blue, 2 yellow, and 1 green.

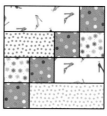 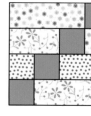

A block.   A block.
Make 2 orange.   Make 5 blue.

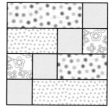 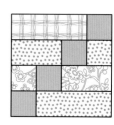

A block.   A block.
Make 2 yellow.   Make 1 green.

Block B

1. Repeat steps 1 and 2 of block A to make the units for four orange, one blue, two yellow, and three green blocks.

2. Rotate the units as shown to make reverse-image blocks for block B. The colored squares will form a diagonal chain in the opposite direction from that in the A blocks. Sew the pieces together to make 10 of block B.

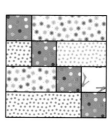 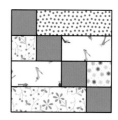

B block.   B block.
Make 4 orange.   Make 1 blue.

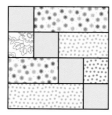 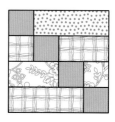

B block.   B block.
Make 2 yellow.   Make 3 green.

Assembling the Quilt Top

1 Arrange alternating A and B blocks in five rows of four blocks each, leaving approximately 2½" between the blocks. Position the blocks as shown in the quilt diagram, or play with the arrangement to come up with your own design.

2 Position the sashing strips and sashing squares (chutes) on two sides of each block as shown. You'll have a few squares and sashing strips left over for the border.

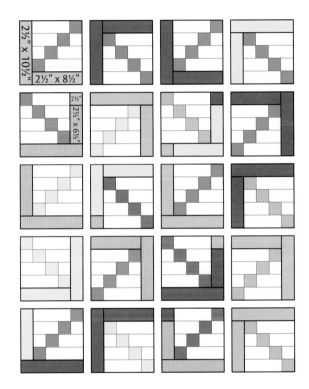

3 Arrange the border pieces around the quilt center. In the quilt shown, some of the sashing fabrics extend into the border. Previewing how everything looks before sewing the sashing to the blocks allows you to make adjustments to the pieces. You may decide to rearrange some of the fabrics, add more prints, or change the directions of the chutes and ladders to make your own unique design.

4 Sew the sashing strips to a block and return it to the layout before sewing the sashing to another block. It's very easy to scramble your design if you try to strip piece all of the sashing pieces to the blocks at once. Always sew the 8½"-long sashing strip to the block first, and then add the 10½"-long strip. Some of the sashing strips are made from a 2½" square and a different-colored

strip. Sew the square to the adjacent strip before sewing the sashing unit to the block. Press the seam allowances toward the sashing strip.

5 Sew the blocks into four columns, each with five blocks and their sashing strips. Press the seam allowances in opposite directions from column to column. Sew the columns together and press the seam allowances in one direction.

6 Sew the border pieces together and press. Sew the side borders to the quilt top and press the seam allowances toward the quilt center. Sew the top and bottom borders to the quilt top and press the seam allowances toward the quilt center.

Finishing the Quilt

Go to ShopMartingale.com/HowtoQuilt if you need more information on finishing techniques.

1 Layer and baste your quilt, and quilt as desired.

2 Using the 2½"-wide binding strips, prepare and attach the binding.

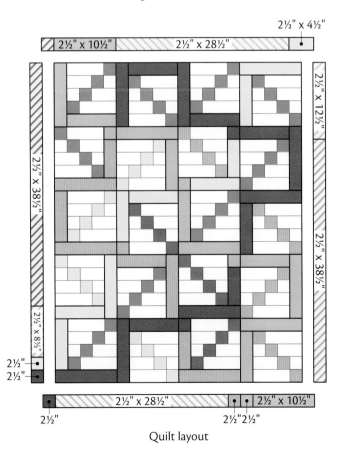

Quilt layout

Kaleidoscope

Kaleidoscopes hold a magical appeal, full of color and pattern and surprise—how will the shapes shift next? Create a kaleidoscopic quilt using eye-popping prints, and open yourself up to the unexpected.

FINISHED QUILT: 40" × 44" • **FINISHED BLOCK:** 4" × 4"

Designed, pieced, and quilted by Kate Henderson

Materials

Yardage is based on 42"-wide fabric.

29 precut strips, 2½" × 42", of assorted prints for blocks and outer border

1½ yards of cream solid for blocks and borders

½ yard of green print for binding

2¾ yards of fabric for backing

46" × 50" piece of batting

VARIETY IS THE SPICE

All the necessary print rectangles can be cut from just 21 strips, but designer Kate Henderson wanted more variety, so she used 29 different fabric strips.

Cutting

From *each* of the 29 print strips, cut:

7 rectangles, 2½" × 4½" (203 total; 21 are extra)

From the cream solid, cut:

13 strips, 2½" × 42"; crosscut into 208 squares, 2½" × 2½"*

4 strips, 2½" × 42"; crosscut into 4 strips, 2½" × 36½"

From the green print, cut:

5 strips, 2½" × 42"

If your fabric is slightly narrower, cut up to 2 additional strips to achieve the right number of squares.

Making the Blocks

Press the seam allowances as indicated by the arrows, or as otherwise instructed.

1. Draw a diagonal line from corner to corner on the wrong side of four cream 2½" squares. Place a marked square on one end of a print 2½" × 4½" rectangle, right sides together and corners aligned. Sew on the line. Trim the excess corner fabric, leaving a ¼" seam allowance, and press. Sew a second marked square to the other end of the rectangle, being careful to position the seam as shown. Repeat with a second matching print rectangle, reversing the seam angles to result in a mirror-image pair. Make 32 pairs (64 total).

Make 32 pairs.

2. Sew together each pair of mirror-image units from step 1. Make 32 blocks.

Make 32.

Assembling the Quilt Top

1. Lay out eight blocks in a row as shown and sew the blocks together. Make four rows.

Make 4.

2. Sew 16 print rectangles together along their long edges. Make five rows.

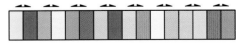

Make 5.

3 Lay out the five rectangle rows and four block rows in alternating positions as shown. Sew the rows together.

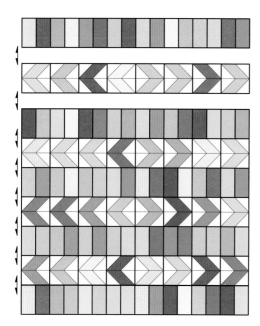

4 Sew cream 2½" × 36½" strips to the sides of the quilt top, and sew the remaining cream strips to the top and bottom of the quilt top to complete the inner border.

5 Draw a diagonal line from corner to corner on the wrong side of two cream 2½" squares. Place a marked square on one end of a print 2½" × 4½" rectangle, right sides together and corners aligned. Sew on the line. Trim the excess corner fabric, leaving a ¼" seam allowance, and press. Repeat on the other end of the rectangle to make a flying-geese unit as shown. Make 38.

Make 38.

6 Sew 10 flying-geese units together to make a side border; make two. Press the seam allowances open. Sew nine flying-geese units together for the top border; add a cream square to each end. Press the seam allowances open. Repeat to make the bottom border.

7 Sew the pieced side borders to the quilt top, orienting the strips as shown, and then add the pieced top and bottom borders.

Quilt assembly

Finishing the Quilt

Go to ShopMartingale.com/HowtoQuilt if you need more information on finishing techniques.

1 Layer and baste your quilt, and quilt as desired.

2 Using the green 2½"-wide strips, prepare and attach the binding.

Pinwheel

/////////////

Kim Brackett confides that this was one of the first quilts she made with 2½" strips cut from her scraps, and after this one, she was hooked. Will you be next to fall under the spell? Try using just two colors: blue and white, red and tan, or pink and yellow.

FINISHED QUILT: 56½" × 68½" • **FINISHED BLOCK:** 12" × 12"

Designed, pieced, and quilted by Kim Brackett

Materials

Yardage is based on 42"-wide fabric.

35 precut strips, 2½" × 42", of assorted light prints for blocks

27 precut strips, 2½" × 42", of assorted dark prints for blocks

⅞ yard of red print for border

⅝ yard of green print for binding

4 yards of fabric for backing

63" × 75" piece of batting

Cutting

From *each* of 12 light print strips, cut:

3 rectangles, 2½" × 6½" (36 total)*

2 rectangles, 2½" × 4½" (24 total)**

4 squares, 2½" × 2½" (48 total)***

From *each* of 12 light print strips, cut:

2 rectangles, 2½" × 6½" (24 total)*

3 rectangles, 2½" × 4½" (36 total)**

4 squares, 2½" × 2½" (48 total)***

From *each* of 11 light print strips, cut:

2 rectangles, 2½" × 6½" (22 total)*

2 rectangles, 2½" × 4½" (22 total)**

6 squares, 2½" × 2½" (66 total)***

From *each* of the 27 dark print strips, cut:

3 rectangles, 2½" × 6½" (81 total; 1 is extra)

3 rectangles, 2½" × 4½" (81 total; 1 is extra)

From the red print, cut:

6 strips, 4½" × 42"

From the green print, cut:

7 strips, 2½" × 42"

There will be a total of 82 light 2½" × 6½" rectangles; 2 will be extra.

**There will be a total of 82 light 2½" × 4½" rectangles; 2 will be extra.*

***There will be a total of 162 light 2½" × 2½" squares; 2 will be extra.*

To cut your blocks from scraps rather than using precut 2½" strips as listed in "Materials" at left, follow these instructions.

From light print scraps, cut:

80 rectangles, 2½" × 6½"

80 rectangles, 2½" × 4½"

160 squares, 2½" × 2½"

From dark print scraps, cut:

80 rectangles, 2½" × 6½"

80 rectangles, 2½" × 4½"

Making the Blocks

Press the seam allowances as indicated by the arrows, or as otherwise instructed.

1 Draw a diagonal line from corner to corner on the wrong side of two light 2½" squares. Place a marked square on each end of a dark 2½" × 6½" rectangle as shown, right sides together and corners aligned. Sew on the lines. Trim the excess corner fabric, leaving a ¼" seam allowance, and press. Make four for each of the 20 blocks.

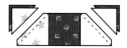 

Make 80.

2 Place a light 2½" × 4½" rectangle at right angles on a dark 2½" × 4½" rectangle, right sides together and corners aligned. Draw a diagonal line on the light rectangle as shown. Sew on the line. Trim the excess corner fabric, leaving a ¼" seam allowance, and press. Make four for each of the 20 blocks.

Make 80.

3 Sew each unit from step 1 to a unit from step 2.

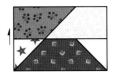

Make 80.

4 Sew a light 2½" × 6½" rectangle to the top of each unit from step 3 as shown. Make four for each of the 20 blocks.

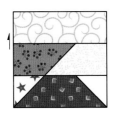

Make 80.

5 Join four of the units from step 4 as shown to complete one block. Carefully clip the seam allowances at the intersection of the units; clip up to, but not through, the stitching. Press the seam allowances in a counterclockwise direction. Make 20 blocks.

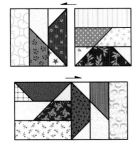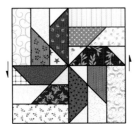

Make 20.

Assembling the Quilt Top

1 Lay out five rows of four blocks each.

2 Sew the blocks together into rows; press. Sew the rows together and press the seam allowances in one direction.

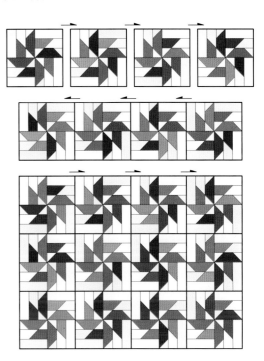

3 Join the red 4½"-wide strips end to end. Measure the length of the quilt top through the center. Cut two strips to that measurement and sew them to the sides of the quilt top. Press the seam allowances toward the borders. Measure the width of the quilt top through the center, including the borders just added. Cut two strips to that measurement and sew them to the top and bottom of the quilt top to complete the border. Press the seam allowances toward the borders.

Finishing the Quilt

Go to ShopMartingale.com/HowtoQuilt if you need more information on finishing techniques.

1 Layer and baste your quilt, and quilt as desired.

2 Using the green 2½"-wide strips, prepare and attach the binding.

Dot Dot Dash

Batik strips line up side by side, with rows of squares judiciously interspersed. The blocks run in alternating directions, but the effect is one of gorgeous simplicity.

FINISHED QUILT: 48½" × 72½" • **FINISHED BLOCK:** 12" × 12"

Designed and pieced by Julie Herman; machine quilted by Angela Walters

Materials

Yardage is based on 42"-wide fabric.
50 precut strips, 2½" × 42", of assorted batiks for blocks
⅔ yard of gray batik for bias binding
3⅓ yards of fabric for backing
55" × 79" piece of batting

Cutting

From 10 of the batik strips, cut a *total* of:
144 squares, 2½" × 2½"

From the remaining 40 batik strips, cut a *total* of:
120 rectangles, 2½" × 12½"

From the gray batik, cut:
255" of 2¼"-wide bias strips

Making the Blocks

Press the seam allowances as indicated by the arrows, or as otherwise instructed.

1. Sew six assorted batik squares together to make a pieced strip. The strip should measure 12½" long. Repeat to make a total of 24 pieced strips.

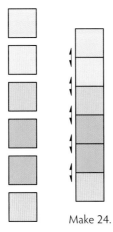

Make 24.

2. Lay out five assorted batik rectangles and one pieced strip as shown. Sew the pieces together to complete the block. Repeat to make 24 blocks.

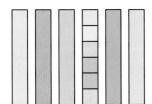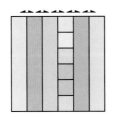

Make 24.

Assembling the Quilt Top

1. Lay out six rows of four blocks each, rotating every other block as shown.

2. Sew the blocks together into rows, and then sew the rows together.

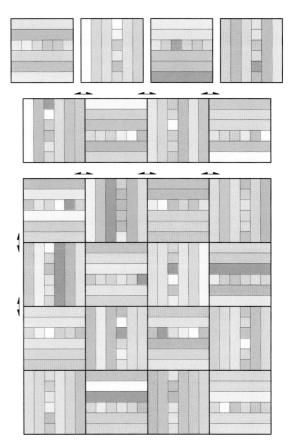

Finishing the Quilt

Go to ShopMartingale.com/HowtoQuilt if you need more information on finishing techniques.

1. Layer and baste your quilt, and quilt as desired.

2. Using the gray 2¼"-wide bias strips, prepare and attach the binding.

Wayfarer

Blending favorite aspects of a Many Trips around the World quilt and the styling of a bargello quilt, this unique design offers plenty of movement. Choose a mix of print values with good contrast to accentuate the design.

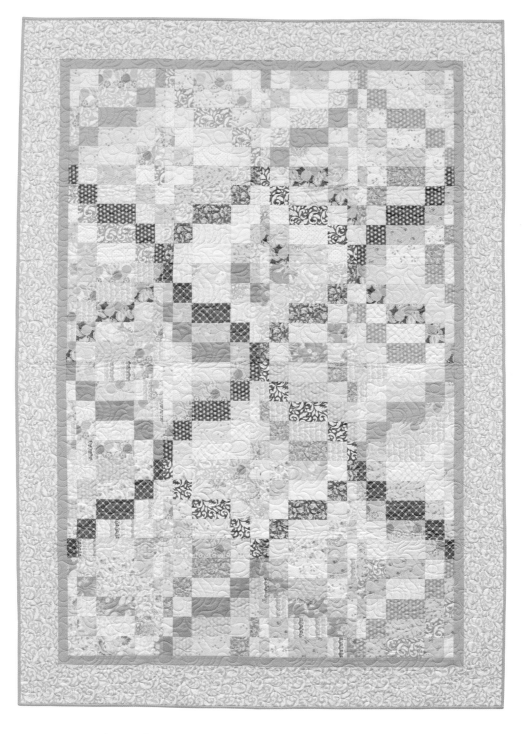

FINISHED QUILT: 50½" × 70½" • **FINISHED BLOCK:** 10" × 10"

Designed, pieced, and quilted by Rebecca Silbaugh

Materials

Yardage is based on 42"-wide fabric.

40 precut strips, 2½" × 42", of assorted light, medium, and dark prints for blocks

⅓ yard of pink dot for inner border

1 yard of green print for outer border

⅝ yard of fabric for binding

3½ yards of fabric for backing

59" × 79" piece of batting

Cutting

From *each* of the 40 light, medium, and dark print strips, cut:

3 strips, 2½" × 14" (120 total)

From the pink dot, cut:

6 strips, 1½" × 42"

From the green print, cut:

7 strips, 4½" × 42"

From the binding fabric, cut:

7 strips, 2¼" × 42"

Making the Blocks

Press the seam allowances as indicated by the arrows, or as otherwise instructed.

1. Randomly select five print 2½" × 14" strips and lay them out as shown, making sure that the strips contrast well with each other. Place the boldest or darkest strip at the bottom of the grouping. Make sure there is good contrast between the top and bottom strips as well.

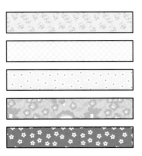

2. Keeping the five strips in order, sew them together to make a strip set. Repeat to make a total of 24 strip sets, 12 with the darkest strip at the bottom and 12 with the darkest strip at the top.

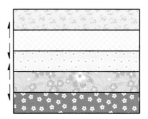

Make 12 of each.

3. Choose 12 strip sets to be A or "up" blocks and 12 to be B or "down" blocks. On each strip set for block A, fold the boldest strip up to match the raw edge of the top strip, right sides together. Stitch along the raw edges to create a tube. Make 12 tubes. Set aside the remaining strip sets for the B blocks.

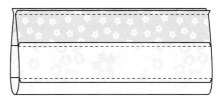

Make 12.

4. Cut each tube across the seam lines, in the order listed, to create segments in the following widths: 1½", 2½", 4½", 2½", and 1½".

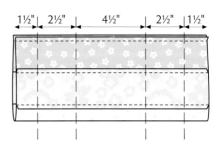

5 Starting with the first 1½"-wide section, remove the line of stitching that created the tube. On the first 2½"-wide section, with the stitching that created the tube at the top and working in a *counterclockwise* direction, remove the next row of stitching. Continuing around the tube in a counterclockwise direction, remove the seam in each of the remaining sections as shown. Keep the five sections in order while you work.

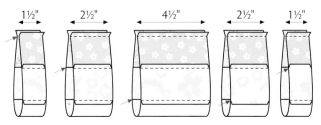

1½" 2½" 4½" 2½" 1½"

Remove seams indicated by red arrows.

6 Once all of the sections are flat, carefully clip the seam allowances of the seam that created the tube (unless the stitching has already been removed), making sure to clip up to, but not through, the stitching. Press the seam allowances in alternating directions as shown. This will help nest the seams when constructing the block later. Again, keep the five sections in order while you work.

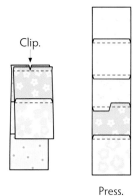

Clip.

Press.

7 Sew the sections together to make a block. Repeat to make a total of 12 A blocks.

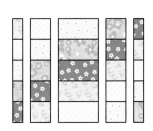 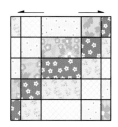

Block A.
Make 12.

8 To create the tube for the B blocks, position the strip set so the boldest strip is at the top. Fold the bottom strip up to meet the raw edge of the boldest strip, right sides together, and stitch the edges together. Make 12 tubes.

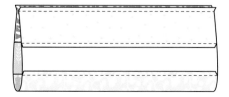

Make 12.

9 Repeat step 4 to cut each tube into sections. Repeat step 5, removing the stitching that created the tube in the first section. Then, working around the sections in a *clockwise* direction, remove the stitching in each of the remaining sections as shown. Keep the five sections in order while you work.

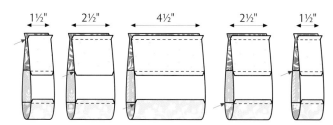

1½" 2½" 4½" 2½" 1½"

Remove seams indicated by red arrows.

10 Once all of the sections are flat, carefully clip the seam allowances of the seam that created the tube (unless the stitching has already been removed). Press the seam allowances in alternating directions as shown. Remember to keep the five sections in order as you work.

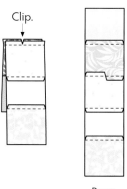

Clip.

Press.

11 Sew the sections together to make a block. Make 12 total of block B.

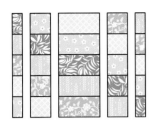 

Block B.
Make 12.

Assembling the Quilt Top

1 Lay out the A and B blocks in six rows of four blocks each, alternating them as shown in the quilt diagram below to mimic a Trip around the World setting.

2 Sew the blocks together into rows, and then sew the rows together.

3 Measure the width of the quilt top through the center. Trim two of the pink-dot 1½"-wide strips to that measurement and sew them to the top and bottom of the quilt top. Join the remaining pink-dot strips end to end. Measure the length of the quilt top through the center, including the borders just added. From the pieced strip, cut two strips to that measurement and sew them to the sides of the quilt top to complete the inner border.

4 Join the green print 4½"-wide strips end to end and repeat step 3 to add the outer border.

Finishing the Quilt

Go to ShopMartingale.com/HowtoQuilt if you need more information on finishing techniques.

1 Layer and baste your quilt, and quilt as desired.

2 Using the 2¼"-wide binding strips, prepare and attach the binding.

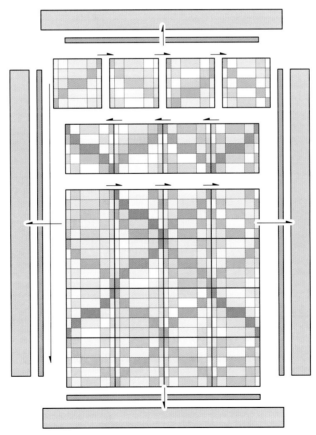

Quilt assembly

Basic Postage

Traditional Postage Stamp quilts are made with tiny 1" squares. Thanks to a slight boost in the size of the squares, plus the addition of alternating larger squares, the process loses its intimidation factor and becomes downright inviting.

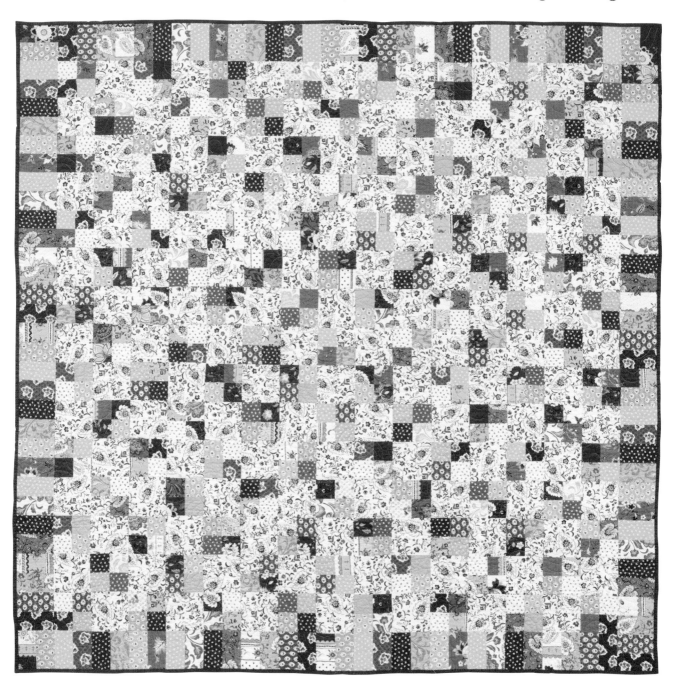

FINISHED QUILT: 69" × 69" • **FINISHED BLOCK:** 12" × 12"

Designed and pieced by Amy Ellis; machine quilted by Natalia Bonner

Materials

Yardage is based on 42"-wide fabric.

40 precut strips, 2½" × 42", of assorted prints for
   blocks and border*

2 yards of white floral for blocks

½ yard of blue print for blocks and border

⅝ yard of red print for binding

4¼ yards of fabric for backing

75" × 75" piece of batting

*Or 3 yards total of assorted prints cut into 40 strips,
2½" × 42"*

Cutting

From the white floral, cut:

14 strips, 4½" × 42"; crosscut into 112 squares,
   4½" × 4½"

From the blue print, cut:

6 strips, 2½" × 42"

From the red print, cut:

7 strips, 2½" × 42"

Making the Blocks

Add the blue 2½" × 42" strips to your mix of assorted
precut strips. Choose 30 of the 46 strips to make strip
sets, and set aside 16 strips for the pieced border.
Press the seam allowances as indicated by the arrows,
or as otherwise instructed.

1 Pin and sew a light and a dark 2½"-wide strip
together. Make 15 strip sets.

Make 15 strip sets.

2 Cut the strip sets into 226 segments, 2½" wide.

Cut 226 segments.

3 Pin, carefully matching the seams, and sew two
segments together to make a four-patch unit.
Repeat to make 113 four-patch units.

Make 113
four-patch units.

4 Pin and sew two four-patch units and one floral
4½" square together as shown. Make 38 of row A.

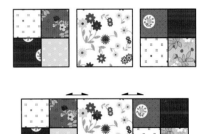

Row A.
Make 38.

5 Pin and sew two floral 4½" squares and one four-
patch unit together as shown. Make 37 of row B.

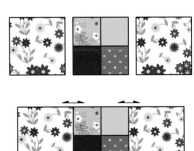

Row B.
Make 37.

6 Pin, carefully matching seams, and sew two of row A and one of row B together to make block 1. Make 13 of block 1 and trim the blocks to 12½" square.

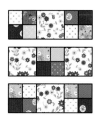 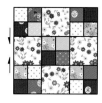

Block 1.
Make 13.

7 Pin, carefully matching seams, and sew two of row B and one of row A together to make block 2. Make 12 of block 2 and trim the blocks to 12½" square.

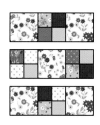 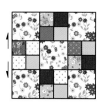

Block 2.
Make 12.

Assembling the Quilt Top

1 Lay out five rows of five blocks each, alternating blocks 1 and 2 as shown.

2 Sew the blocks together into rows; press. Sew the rows together and press the seam allowances in one direction.

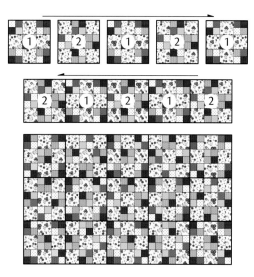

3 Sew four assorted 2½"-wide strips together to make a strip set. Make four strip sets. Cut each strip set into eight segments, 4½" wide.

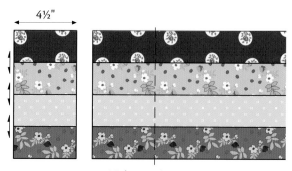

4½"

Make 4 strip sets.
Cut 8 segments from each (32 total).

4 Sew eight segments together to make a border. Make four borders.

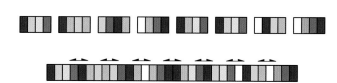

5 Sew a pieced border to one side of the quilt top, stopping halfway.

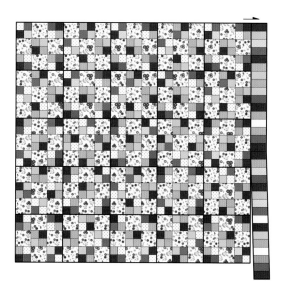

6 Working counterclockwise, sew the remaining borders to the sides of the quilt top. Finish sewing the first border to the quilt to complete the quilt top.

Finishing the Quilt

Go to ShopMartingale.com/HowtoQuilt if you need more information on finishing techniques.

1 Layer and baste your quilt, and quilt as desired.

2 Using the red 2½"-wide strips, prepare and attach the binding.

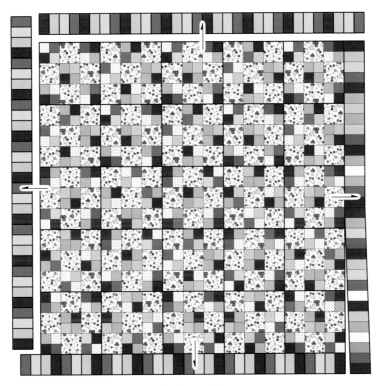

Quilt assembly

Fat Man's Squeeze

A long-ago family trip to Tennessee included a walk through immense, ancient rock formations, including a narrow passage called Fat Man's Squeeze. Kathy Brown says the centers of these blocks remind her of that unforgettable—and unforgettably named—attraction.

FINISHED QUILT: 43" × 53" • **FINISHED BLOCK:** 10" × 10"

Designed by Kathy Brown; pieced by Kathy Brown and Janell Crosslin; quilted by Carol Hilton

Materials

Yardage is based on 42"-wide fabric.

32 precut strips, 2½" × 42", of assorted red, light blue, tan, navy, and cream* prints for blocks

¾ yard of navy print for inner border

2⅛ yards of cream floral for outer border and binding

2⅞ yards of fabric for backing

51" × 61" piece of batting

In the quilt shown, Kathy cut one cream strip from the floral border fabric.

Cutting

From the navy print, cut:

8 strips, 2" × 42"

From the cream floral, cut:

8 strips, 5½" × 42"

8 strips, 2½" × 42"

Making the Blocks

Press the seam allowances as indicated by the arrows, or as otherwise instructed.

1. From your 2½" strips, choose:
   - 4 assorted red strips
   - 4 assorted light blue strips
   - 8 assorted tan strips
   - 8 assorted navy strips
   - 8 assorted cream strips

2. With right sides together, sew a red strip to a tan strip. Make a total of four strip sets. Repeat to make a total of four tan/navy strip sets, four cream/navy strip sets, and four cream/light blue strip sets.

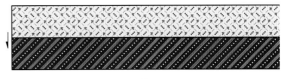

Make 4.

Make 4.

Make 4.

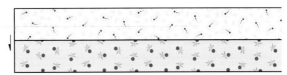

Make 4.

3. Referring to "Cutting Triangles" on page 9, cut six 90° double-strip triangles from each strip set.

4. Lay a 90° triangle face up on your cutting mat. Place a 6" square ruler on the triangle, lining up the bottom edge of the ruler with the bottom raw edge of the triangle, and the right edge of the 6" ruler with the top of the triangle.

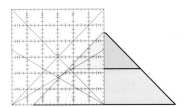

5 Using a rotary cutter, cut the triangle in half along the edge of the 6" ruler, creating two mirror-image triangles. Repeat with the remaining 90° triangles and arrange 16 sets of 12 triangles each:
- tan tip/red strip pointing left
- tan tip/red strip pointing right
- red tip/tan strip pointing left
- red tip/tan strip pointing right
- tan tip/navy strip pointing left
- tan tip/navy strip pointing right
- navy tip/tan strip pointing left
- navy tip/tan strip pointing right
- cream tip/navy strip pointing left
- cream tip/navy strip pointing right
- navy tip/cream strip pointing left
- navy tip/cream strip pointing right
- cream tip/light blue strip pointing left
- cream tip/light blue strip pointing right
- light blue tip/cream strip pointing left
- light blue tip/cream strip pointing right

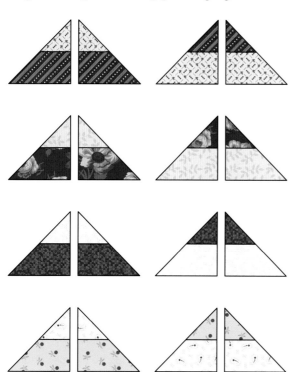

6 With right sides together, sew a tan-tip/red-strip-pointing-left triangle to a red-tip/tan-strip-pointing-right triangle. Repeat to make a second unit. Sew the two units together to make a square. Repeat to make a second square.

Make 2.

7 With right sides together, sew a red-tip/tan-strip-pointing-left triangle to a tan-tip/red-strip-pointing-right triangle. Repeat to make a second unit. Sew the two units together to make a square. Repeat to make a second square. Rotate each of these squares 90° to the right.

Make 2.
Rotate 90°.

8 Lay out the squares, placing the two squares from step 6 in the upper-left and lower-right positions and the two squares from step 7 in the upper-right and lower-left positions. Sew the top squares together, and then sew the bottom squares together. Sew the top unit to the bottom unit to make one block.

9 Repeat steps 6–8 to make a total of three red/tan blocks. Starch each block to preserve the bias edges of the triangles.

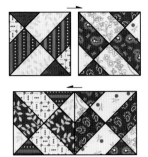

Make 3.

10 Repeat to make a total of three tan/navy blocks, three cream/navy blocks, and three cream/light blue blocks.

Make 3.   Make 3.

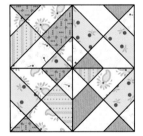

Make 3.

Assembling the Quilt Top

1 Lay out four rows of three blocks each, orienting the blocks as shown.

2 Sew the blocks together into rows; press. Sew the rows together and press the seam allowances in one direction. Stitch around the perimeter ⅛"

from the raw edges to stabilize the bias edges of the quilt top.

3 Join two navy 2"-wide strips end to end. Repeat to make a total of four pieced strips. Measure the length of the quilt top through the center. Trim two pieced strips to that measurement and sew them to the sides of the quilt top. Press the seam allowances away from the center. Measure the width of the quilt top through the center, including the borders just added. Trim the two remaining pieced strips to that measurement and sew them to the top and bottom of the quilt top to complete the inner border. Press the seam allowances away from the center.

4 Repeat with the floral 5½"-wide strips to add the outer border.

Finishing the Quilt

Go to ShopMartingale.com/HowtoQuilt if you need more information on finishing techniques.

1 Layer and baste your quilt, and quilt as desired.

2 Using the floral 2½"-wide strips, prepare and attach the binding.

Purple Daze

Purple is often associated with royalty. It's hard not to feel regal when working with such a gorgeous shade of purple! This quilt includes wonderful Star blocks and the opportunity to put your favorite batiks on display.

FINISHED QUILT: 67½" × 79½" • **FINISHED BLOCKS:** 6" × 6" and 18" × 18"

Designed, pieced, and quilted by Cheryl Brown

Materials

Yardage is based on 42"-wide fabric.

40 precut strips, 2½" × 42", of assorted batiks for Square-in-a-Square blocks

2 yards of dark purple batik for Star blocks and outer border

1½ yards of yellow-and-pink batik for Star block backgrounds

⅞ yard of beige batik for inner border and border corner blocks

⅞ yard of purple-striped batik for bias binding

5¼ yards of fabric for backing

74" × 86" piece of batting

Cutting

From the 40 batik strips, cut a *total* of:

63 squares, 2½" × 2½"

63 matching sets of 2 squares, 2½" × 2½", and 2 rectangles, 2½" × 6½"

From the dark purple batik, cut:

3 strips, 5⅜" × 42"; crosscut into 16 squares, 5⅜" × 5⅜"

1 strip, 5" × 42"; crosscut into 4 squares, 5" × 5"

1 strip, 3⅜" × 42"; crosscut into 8 squares, 3⅜" × 3⅜"

2 strips, 3⅛" × 42"; crosscut into 16 squares, 3⅛" × 3⅛"

6 strips, 5½" × 42"

From the yellow-and-pink batik, cut:

4 squares, 10¼" × 10¼"

1 strip, 5¾" × 42"; crosscut into 4 squares, 5¾" × 5¾"

2 strips, 5" × 42"; crosscut into 16 squares, 5" × 5"

2 strips, 2¾" × 42"; crosscut into 16 squares, 2¾" × 2¾"

From the beige batik, cut:

2 squares, 6¼" × 6¼"

1 strip, 5½" × 42"; crosscut into 4 squares, 5½" × 5½"

7 strips, 2" × 42"

From the purple-striped batik, cut:

310" of 2¼"-wide bias strips

Making the Square-in-a-Square Blocks

Each block is made with two fabrics, one for the center square and a contrasting fabric for the outer squares and rectangles. Press the seam allowances as indicated by the arrows, or as otherwise instructed.

1 Sew matching 2½" squares to opposite sides of a 2½" center square.

2 Sew matching 2½" × 6½" rectangles to the top and bottom of the unit as shown. Make 63 Square-in-a-Square blocks.

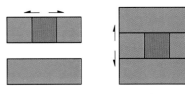

Make 63.

Making the Star Blocks

1 Draw a diagonal line from corner to corner on the wrong side of each dark purple 3⅛" square.

2 Place two marked squares on opposite corners of a yellow-and-pink 5¾" square, right sides together. Sew ¼" from the drawn line on both sides. Cut on the drawn line; press.

3 Place a marked dark purple square on the yellow-and-pink corner of each half from step 2, right sides together. Sew ¼" from the drawn line on both sides. Cut on the drawn line; press. This will give you four flying-geese units.

4 Sew flying-geese units to opposite sides of a dark purple 5" square; press. Sew a yellow-and-pink 2¾" square to each end of the two remaining flying-geese units; press. Sew these units to the top and bottom of the block to complete the center of the larger block.

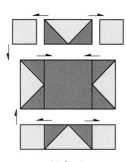

Make 4.

5 Draw a diagonal line from corner to corner on the wrong side of each dark purple 5⅜" square. Place two marked squares on opposite corners of a yellow-and-pink 10¼" square, right sides together. Sew ¼" from the drawn line on both sides. Cut on the drawn line; press.

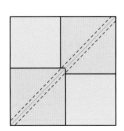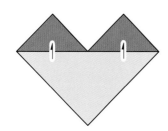

6 Place a marked dark purple square on the yellow-and-pink corner of each half from step 5, right sides together. Sew ¼" from the drawn line on both sides. Cut on the drawn line; press. This will give you four flying-geese units.

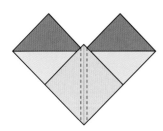

7 Sew flying-geese units to opposite sides of the block center; press. Sew a yellow-and-pink 5" square to each end of the two remaining flying-geese units; press. Sew these units to the top and bottom of the block. Make four Star blocks.

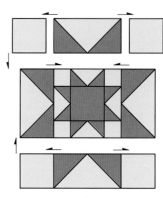

Make 4.

Assembling the Quilt Top

1 Lay out the blocks in rows and sections as shown in the quilt diagram on page 131, alternating light and dark blocks as much as possible.

2 Sew the blocks together into sections, and then sew the sections together.

3 Join the beige 2"-wide strips end to end. Measure the width of the quilt top through the center and cut two strips to that length. Sew the strips to the top and bottom of the quilt top and press the seam allowances toward the border. Measure the length of the quilt top, including the borders just added, and cut two strips to that length. Sew the strips to the sides of the quilt top. The quilt should measure 57½" × 69½".

4 Draw a diagonal line from corner to corner on the wrong side of each dark purple 3⅜" square. Place two marked squares on opposite corners of a beige 6¼" square, right sides together. Sew ¼" from the drawn line on both sides. Cut on the drawn line; press.

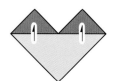

5 Place a marked dark purple square on the beige corner of each half from step 4, right sides together. Sew ¼" from the drawn line on both sides. Cut on the drawn line; press. This will give you four flying-geese units. Make eight flying-geese units.

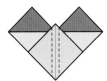

Make 8.

6 Join the dark purple 5½"-wide strips end to end. Cut two strips, 52½" long, for the top and bottom borders and two strips, 64½" long, for the side borders.

7 Sew a flying-geese unit to each end of each border strip. Add a beige 5½" square to each end of the strips for the top and bottom borders.

Top and bottom borders

Side borders

8 Sew the pieced outer-border strips to the sides and then to the top and bottom of the quilt top.

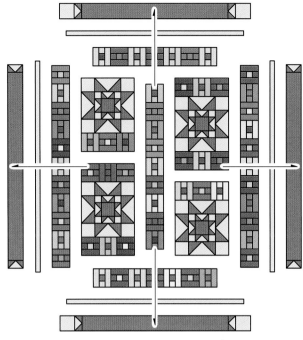

Quilt assembly

Finishing the Quilt

Go to ShopMartingale.com/HowtoQuilt if you need more information on finishing techniques.

1 Layer and baste your quilt, and quilt as desired.

2 Using the striped 2¼"-wide bias strips, prepare and attach the binding.

Flowers for Nana Girl

When quilter Karen Williamson became a grandmother, she asked to be called "Nana," but it wasn't long after her granddaughter learned to talk that the child began calling Karen "Nana Girl."

FINISHED QUILT: 56½" × 66½" • **FINISHED BLOCK:** 8" × 8"

Designed by Kim Brackett; pieced and quilted by Karen Williamson

Materials

Yardage is based on 42"-wide fabric.

20 precut strips, 2½" × 42", of assorted dark prints in pinks, reds, browns, and golds for blocks

2 yards of pale yellow marbled print for blocks, sashing strips, and sashing squares

½ yard of green print for sashing-strip "leaves"

⅜ yard of brown print for inner border

1⅓ yards of large-scale floral for outer border

⅝ yard of pink print for binding

4 yards of fabric for backing

63" × 73" piece of batting

Cutting

From *each* of the 20 dark print strips, cut:

8 rectangles, 2½" × 4½" (160 total)

From the pale yellow marbled print, cut:

13 strips, 2½" × 42"; crosscut into 49 rectangles, 2½" × 8½"

12 strips, 2½" × 42"; crosscut into 190 squares, 2½" × 2½"

From the green print, cut:

6 strips, 2½" × 42"; crosscut into 80 squares, 2½" × 2½"

From the brown print, cut:

5 strips, 2" × 42"

From the large-scale floral, cut:

7 strips, 6" × 42"

From the pink print, cut:

7 strips, 2½" × 42"

CUTTING FROM YOUR STASH

Time to whittle down your fabric stash? To cut your blocks from scraps rather than using precut 2½" strip as listed in "Materials" at left, follow these instructions.

From assorted pink, red, brown, and gold prints, cut:

20 sets of 8 rectangles, 2½" × 4½" (160 total)

From assorted green prints, cut:

80 squares, 2½" × 2½"

From assorted light prints, cut:

49 rectangles, 2½" × 8½"

190 squares, 2½" × 2½"

Making the Blocks

Press the seam allowances as indicated by the arrows, or as otherwise instructed.

1. Draw a diagonal line from corner to corner on the wrong side of two pale yellow 2½" squares. Place a marked square on end of a dark 2½" × 4½" rectangle, right sides together and corners aligned. Sew on the line. Trim the excess corner fabric, leaving a ¼" seam allowance, and press. Sew the second marked square to the other end of the rectangle, being careful to position the seam as shown. Make four identical units for each of the 20 blocks.

Make 4
for each block.

2. Sew a matching 2½" × 4½" rectangle to the top of each unit from step 1.

Make 4
for each block.

3 Sew together four matching units from step 2 as shown. Make 20 blocks.

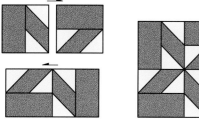

Make 20.

Making the Sashing Strips

1 Referring to the technique used in step 1 of "Making the Blocks" on page 133, place a marked green 2½" square on one end of a pale yellow 2½" × 8½" rectangle. Stitch, trim, and press. Make 18.

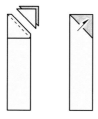

Make 18.

2 In the same manner, place marked green 2½" squares on both ends of a pale yellow 2½" × 8½" rectangle, paying careful attention to the direction of the sewing lines. Stitch, trim, and press. Make 31.

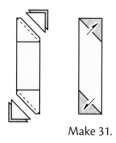

Make 31.

Assembling the Quilt Top

1 Arrange the blocks, pieced sashing strips, and pale yellow 2½" sashing squares as shown.

2 Sew the pieces together into rows; press. Sew the rows together and press the seam allowances in one direction.

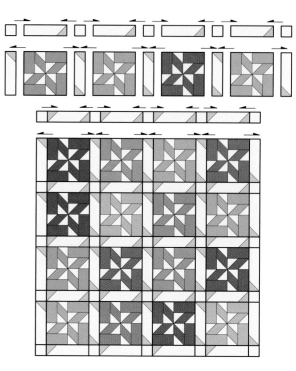

3 Join the brown 2"-wide strips end to end. Measure the length of the quilt top through the center. Cut two strips to that measurement and sew them to the sides of the quilt top. Press the seam allowances away from the center. Measure the width of the quilt top through the center, including the borders just added. Cut two strips to that measurement and sew them to the top and bottom of the quilt top to complete the inner border. Press the seam allowances away from the center.

4 Repeat with the floral 6"-wide strips. The quilt shown features mitered corners in the outer border; visit ShopMartingale.com/HowtoQuilt for detailed instructions.

Finishing the Quilt

Go to ShopMartingale.com/HowtoQuilt if you need more information on finishing techniques.

1 Layer and baste your quilt, and quilt as desired.

2 Using the pink 2½"-wide strips, prepare and attach the binding.

Butterflies

//////////////

There is nothing happier than seeing butterflies fluttering around the garden. Invite the joy indoors with this quilt and have easy-to-piece butterflies fluttering about whenever you please.

FINISHED QUILT: 60" × 60" • **FINISHED BLOCK:** 12" × 12"

Designed, pieced, and quilted by Kate Henderson

Materials

Yardage is based on 42"-wide fabric.

38 precut strips, 2½" × 42", of assorted prints for blocks

2⅓ yards of white solid for blocks

⅝ yard of pink print for binding

3⅞ yards of fabric for backing

66" × 66" piece of batting

Cutting

From *each* of 25 print strips, cut:
2 rectangles, 2½" × 12½" (50 total)
1 rectangle, 2½" × 10½" (25 total)

From *each* of 13 print strips, cut:
4 rectangles, 2½" × 8½" (52 total; 2 are extra)

From the white solid, cut:
19 strips, 2½" × 42"; crosscut into:
    100 rectangles, 2½" × 4½"
    100 squares, 2½" × 2½"
20 strips, 1½" × 42"; crosscut into:
    50 rectangles, 1½" × 12½"
    50 rectangles, 1½" × 2½"

From the pink print, cut:
7 strips, 2½" × 42"

Making the Blocks

Press the seam allowances as indicated by the arrows, or as otherwise instructed.

1 Draw a diagonal line from corner to corner on the wrong side of two white 2½" squares. Place a marked square on each end of a print 2½" × 12½" rectangle as shown, right sides together and corners aligned. Sew on the lines. Trim the excess corner fabric, leaving ¼" seam allowances, and press. Make two from matching print rectangles.

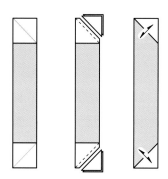

2 Place a white 2½" × 4½" rectangle at right angles on a print 2½" × 8½" rectangle, right sides together and corners aligned. Draw a diagonal line on the white rectangle as shown. Stitch and trim as in step 1. Repeat with a second white rectangle at the other end of the print rectangle, being careful to orient the seam lines as shown. Make two from matching print rectangles.

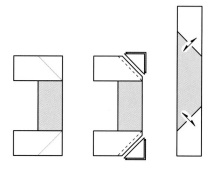

3 Sew a white 1½" × 2½" rectangle to each end of a print 2½" × 10½" rectangle.

4 Arrange the units from steps 1–3 as shown and sew them together. Sew white 1½" × 12½" rectangles to opposite sides of the block. Make 25 blocks.

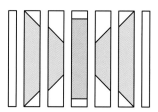 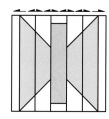

Make 25.

Assembling the Quilt Top

1 Lay out five rows of five blocks each, rotating every other block as shown.

2 Sew the blocks together into rows, and then sew the rows together.

Finishing the Quilt

Go to ShopMartingale.com/HowtoQuilt if you need more information on finishing techniques.

1 Layer and baste your quilt, and quilt as desired.

2 Using the pink 2½"-wide strips, prepare and attach the binding.

Quilt assembly

Under the Sea

Bold geometric shapes mix with a playfully scrappy look. This quilt is intriguing because it's made of just one block, but when the blocks are put together, they form three different designs across the quilt top.

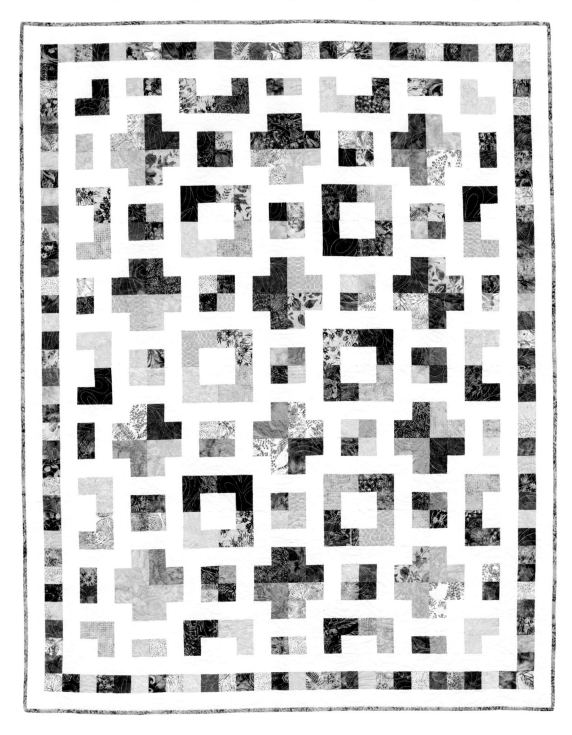

FINISHED QUILT: 60½" × 76½" • **FINISHED BLOCK:** 16" × 16"

Designed, pieced, and quilted by Sue Pfau

Materials

Yardage is based on 42"-wide fabric.

38 precut strips, 2½" × 42", of assorted prints in blues and greens for blocks and pieced middle border

3 yards of white fabric for blocks and inner and outer borders

⅔ yard of fabric for binding

4¾ yards of fabric for backing

69" × 85" piece of batting

Cutting

From *each* of 20 print strips, cut:

1 strip, 2½" × 13" (20 total)

5 rectangles, 2½" × 4½" (100 total; 4 are extra)

From the remaining scraps and 18 print strips, cut a *total* of:

48 rectangles, 2½" × 5½"

32 strips, 2½" × 10¼"

From the white fabric, cut:

39 strips, 2½" × 42"; crosscut *26 strips* into:

96 rectangles, 2½" × 4½"

20 strips, 2½" × 13"

48 rectangles, 2½" × 5½"

From the binding fabric, cut:

8 strips, 2½" × 42"

Making the Blocks

Press the seam allowances as indicated by the arrows, or as otherwise instructed.

1 Sew a print 2½" × 13" strip to a white 2½" × 13" strip along the long edges. Make 20 strip sets and cut them into 96 segments, 2½" wide.

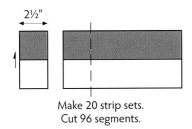

2½"

Make 20 strip sets.
Cut 96 segments.

CUTTING STRAIGHT

When cutting strip sets into smaller segments, align one of the lines on your ruler with a seam of the strip set. This way you will have a "squared off" cut every time.

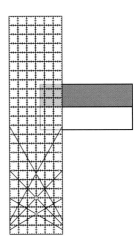

2 Sew a matching 2½" × 4½" rectangle to the segment from step 1 to make unit A. Make sure the pieced segment is on the right with the white square on top. Make 96 units.

Unit A.
Make 96.

3 Sew a print 2½" × 5½" rectangle to a white 2½" × 5½" rectangle along the long edges as shown. Make 48 strip sets and cut them into 96 segments, 2½" wide.

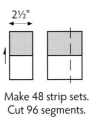

2½"

Make 48 strip sets.
Cut 96 segments.

4 Sew a white 2½" × 4½" rectangle to the segment from step 3 to make unit B. Make sure the pieced segment is on the right with the white square on top. Make 96 units.

Unit B.
Make 96.

5 Sew a unit A and a unit B together exactly as shown. Make 48.

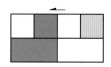

Make 48.

6 Sew a unit A and a unit B together exactly as shown. Make 48.

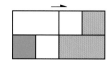

Make 48.

7 Sew one unit from step 5 and one unit from step 6 together as shown to make a quarter of a block. Make 48.

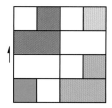

Make 48.

TAMING TRICKY SEAMS

If the seam allowances are pressed in the same directions when you sew the segments or blocks of this quilt together, pin them in the opposite direction. Then, after you sew the segments together, snip the fabric in the seam allowances just below the sewn intersection and press the seam allowances back to their original position.

8 Sew four quarter blocks together exactly as shown. Make 12 blocks. The blocks should measure 16½" square.

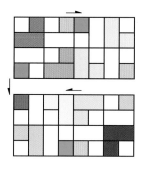
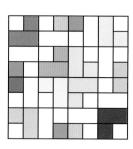

Make 12.

Assembling the Quilt Top

1 Lay out four rows of three blocks each.

2 Sew the blocks together into rows; press. Sew the rows together and press the seam allowances in one direction.

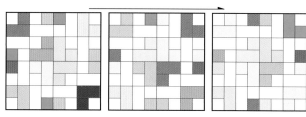

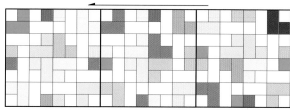

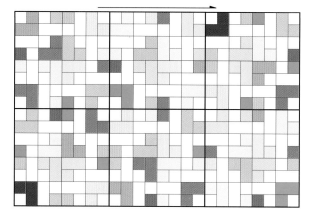

3 Join six white 2½" × 42" strips end to end using diagonal seams. Cut two strips, 64½" long, and two strips, 52½" long. Sew the longer strips to the sides of the quilt top and sew the shorter strips to the top and bottom to complete the inner border.

4 Sew the print 2½" × 10¼" strips together lengthwise in pairs, creating many different color combinations. Press the seam allowances toward the darker fabrics. Make 16 strip sets and cut them into 62 segments, 2½" wide, for the pieced border.

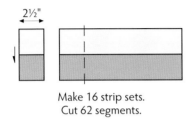

2½"

Make 16 strip sets.
Cut 62 segments.

5 Join 17 border segments end to end. Make two. Sew the pieced strips to the sides of the quilt top.

6 Join 14 border segments end to end. Make two. Sew the pieced strips to the top and bottom of the quilt top to complete the middle border.

7 Join the remaining seven white 2½" × 42" strips end to end using diagonal seams. Cut two strips, 72½" long, and two strips, 60½" long. Sew the longer strips to the sides of the quilt top and sew the shorter strips to the top and bottom to complete the outer border.

Finishing the Quilt

Go to ShopMartingale.com/HowtoQuilt if you need more information on finishing techniques.

1 Layer and baste your quilt, and quilt as desired.

2 Using the 2½"-wide binding strips, prepare and attach the binding.

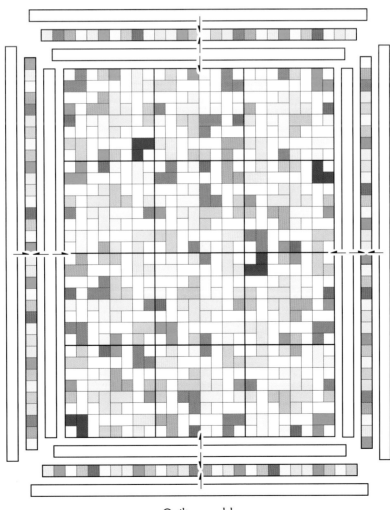

Quilt assembly

Over and Under

Using a solid white background allows even large-scale prints to stand out, and it provides a crisp, clean contrast for the main fabrics.

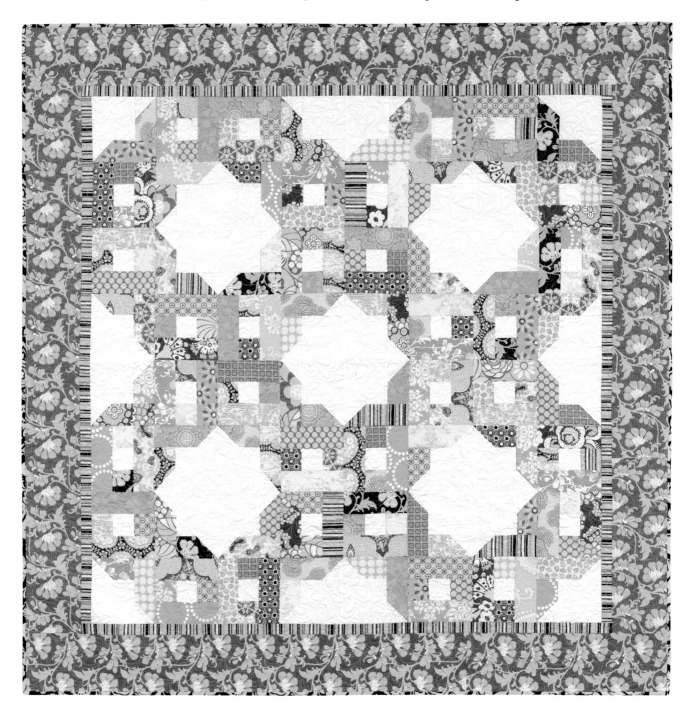

FINISHED QUILT: 61½" × 61½" • **FINISHED BLOCK:** 12" × 12"

Designed, pieced, and quilted by Kim Brackett

Materials

Yardage is based on 42"-wide fabric.

26 precut strips, 2½" × 42", of assorted dark prints in blues and greens for blocks

1⅛ yards of white solid for blocks

⅓ yard of blue-and-green stripe for inner border

1⅛ yards of large-scale floral for outer border

⅝ yard of blue-and-green print for binding

4¼ yards of fabric for backing

68" × 68" piece of batting

Cutting

From *each* of 20 dark print strips, cut:

4 rectangles, 2½" × 6½" (80 total; 2 are extra)

1 rectangle, 2½" × 4½" (20 total)

2 squares, 2½" × 2½" (40 total)

From *each* of 6 dark print strips, cut:

3 rectangles, 2½" × 6½" (18 total)

2 rectangles, 2½" × 4½" (12 total)

4 squares, 2½" × 2½" (24 total)

From the white solid, cut:

4 strips, 4½" × 42"; crosscut into 32 squares, 4½" × 4½"

7 strips, 2½" × 42"; crosscut into 96 squares, 2½" × 2½"

From the blue-and-green stripe, cut:

5 strips, 1½" × 42"

From the large-scale floral, cut:

6 strips, 6" × 42"

From the blue-and-green print, cut:

7 strips, 2½" × 42"

CUTTING FROM YOUR STASH

Time to whittle down your fabric stash? To cut your blocks from scraps rather than using precut 2½" strips as listed in "Materials" at left, follow these instructions.

From assorted blue and green prints, cut:

96 rectangles, 2½" × 6½"

32 rectangles, 2½" × 4½"

64 squares, 2½" × 2½"

From assorted light prints, cut:

32 squares, 4½" × 4½"

96 squares, 2½" × 2½"

Making the Blocks

Press the seam allowances as indicated by the arrows, or as otherwise instructed.

1 Draw a diagonal line from corner to corner on the wrong side of a white 2½" square. Place the marked square on one end of a blue or green 2½" × 4½" rectangle, right sides together and corners aligned. Sew on the line. Trim the excess corner fabric, leaving a ¼" seam allowance, and press. Make 32.

Make 32.

2 Sew a unit from step 1 to a white 4½" square as shown. Make 32.

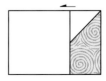

Make 32.

3 Referring to the technique in step 1, place a marked white 2½" square on one end of a blue or green 2½" × 6½" rectangle. Stitch, trim, and press. Make 32.

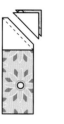

Make 32.

4 Sew a unit from step 3 to a unit from step 2 as shown. Make 32.

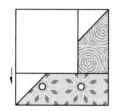

Make 32.

5 Sew blue or green 2½" squares to the top and bottom of a white 2½" square. Make 32.

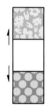

Make 32.

6 Sew blue or green 2½" × 6½" rectangles to opposite sides of a unit from step 5. Make 32.

 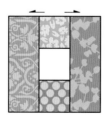

Make 32.

7 Sew together two units from step 4 and two units from step 6 as shown. Carefully clip the seam allowances at the intersection of the units; clip up to, but not through, the stitching. Press the seam allowances in a clockwise direction. Make 16 blocks.

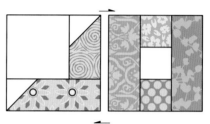

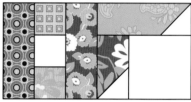

Make 16.

Assembling the Quilt Top

1 Lay out four rows of four blocks each, orienting the blocks as shown.

2 Sew the blocks together into rows; press. Sew the rows together and press the seam allowances in one direction.

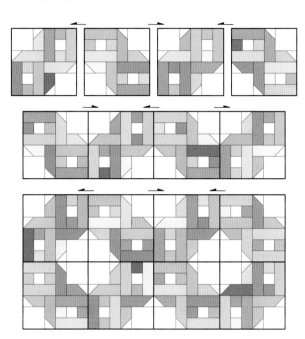

3 Join the blue-and-green striped 1½"-wide strips end to end. Measure the length of the quilt top through the center. Cut two strips to that measurement and sew them to the sides of the quilt top. Press the seam allowances away from the center. Measure the width of the quilt top through the center, including the borders just added. Cut two strips to that measurement and sew them to the top and bottom of the quilt top to complete the inner border. Press the seam allowances away from the center.

4 Repeat with the floral 6"-wide strips to add the outer border.

Finishing the Quilt

Go to ShopMartingale.com/HowtoQuilt if you need more information on finishing techniques.

1 Layer and baste your quilt, and quilt as desired.

2 Using the blue-and-green print 2½"-wide strips, prepare and attach the binding.

Twisted Bars

This quilt works equally well with precut fabrics or with scraps you've saved from various projects. The corner triangles unite the blocks, and the borders continue the scrappy theme.

FINISHED QUILT: 66" × 78" • **FINISHED BLOCK:** 12" × 12"

Designed and pieced by Amy Ellis; machine quilted by Natalia Bonner

Materials

Yardage is based on 42"-wide fabric.

66 precut strips, 2½" × 42", of assorted prints for blocks and pieced outer border*

¾ yard of aqua print for blocks

1 yard of brown solid for inner border and binding

4½ yards of fabric for backing

72" × 84" piece of batting

Or 5 yards total of assorted prints cut into 66 strips, 2½" × 42"

Cutting

From the aqua print, cut:

5 strips, 4½" × 42"; crosscut into 40 squares, 4½" × 4½"

From the brown solid, cut:

8 strips, 1½" × 42"

8 strips, 2½" × 42"

Making the Blocks

Press the seam allowances as indicated by the arrows, or as otherwise instructed.

1 Pin and sew six assorted 2½"-wide strips together. Make seven strip sets.

Make 7 strip sets.

2 Measure the width of the pressed strip sets. They should measure 12½"; if not, it's OK. Just make note of the width. Cut 20 squares, 12½" × 12½", or the measurement of your strip sets.

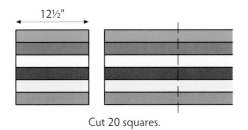

12½"

Cut 20 squares.

3 Draw a diagonal line from corner to corner on the wrong side of the aqua 4½" squares. Place two marked squares on diagonally opposite corners of a pieced 12½" square as shown, right sides together and corners aligned. Sew on the lines. Trim the excess corner fabric, leaving ¼" seam allowances, and press the seam allowances open. Make 20. Trim the blocks to 12½" square.

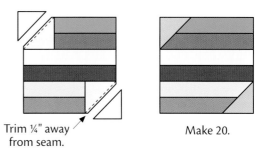

Trim ¼" away from seam.   Make 20.

Assembling the Quilt Top

1 Lay out five rows of four blocks each, orienting the blocks as shown or in another arrangement as desired.

2 Sew the blocks together into rows; press. Sew the rows together and press the seam allowances in one direction.

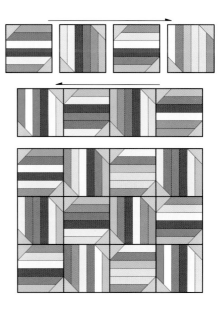

3 Join two brown 1½"-wide strips end to end. Repeat to make a total of four pieced strips. Measure the length of the quilt top through the center. Trim two pieced strips to that measurement and sew them to the sides of the quilt top. Press the seam allowances away from the center. Measure the width of the quilt top through the center, including the borders just added. Trim the two remaining pieced strips to that measurement and sew them to the top and bottom of the quilt top to complete the inner border. Press the seam allowances away from the center.

4 Join the remaining print 2½"-wide strips in pairs end to end. Repeat step 3 to add three more borders one at a time to the quilt top, measuring and trimming the strips to fit. Stagger the seams as you add borders to the sides of the quilt top, and then to the top and bottom.

Finishing the Quilt

Go to ShopMartingale.com/HowtoQuilt if you need more information on finishing techniques.

1 Layer and baste your quilt, and quilt as desired.

2 Using the brown 2½"-wide strips, prepare and attach the binding.

Flair

This design is simple enough that the quilt goes together fairly quickly, but the unusual setting captivates the eye. Sleek gray background strips allow the pretty prints to really pop.

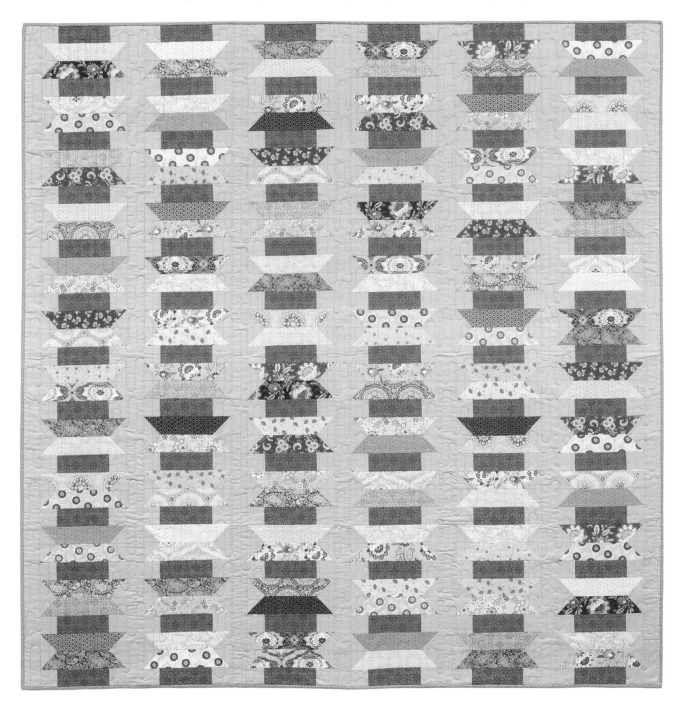

FINISHED QUILT: 74" × 74½" • **FINISHED BLOCK:** 4" × 10"

Designed and pieced by Susan Guzman; machine quilted by Linda Barrett

Materials

Yardage is based on 42"-wide fabric.
36 precut strips, 2½" × 42", of assorted prints for blocks
3⅛ yards of gray solid for blocks and sashing
1 yard of orange print for sashing
⅝ yard of pink print for binding
7⅜ yards of fabric for backing
82" × 83" piece of batting

Cutting

From *each* of the 36 print strips, cut:
4 rectangles, 2½" × 10½" (144 total; A)

From the orange print, cut:
5 strips, 6½" × 42"; crosscut into 78 rectangles, 2½" × 6½" (B)

From the gray solid, cut on the *lengthwise* grain:
16 strips, 2½" × 74½"; crosscut 9 *strips* into 261 squares, 2½" × 2½" (C)

From the remaining gray solid, cut on the *crosswise* grain:
12 strips, 2½" × 42"; crosscut into 183 squares, 2½" × 2½" (C)

From the pink print, cut:
8 strips, 2¼" × 42"

Making the Blocks

Press the seam allowances as indicated by the arrows, or as otherwise instructed.

1 Sew together one orange B rectangle and two gray C squares as shown to make a sashing unit. Make a total of 78 units.

Make 78.

2 Draw a diagonal line from corner to corner on the wrong side of each remaining gray C square. Place a marked square on one end of a print A rectangle. Sew along the marked line. Trim away the corner fabric, leaving a ¼" seam allowance. Press. Place a marked square on the opposite end of the rectangle. Sew, trim, and press to make one unit. Make a total of 144 units.

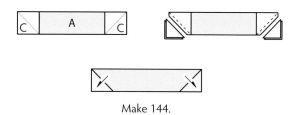

Make 144.

3 Sew two units from step 2 together as shown to make a block. Make a total of 72 blocks.

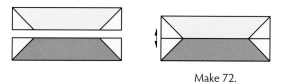

Make 72.

Assembling the Quilt Top

1 Sew 13 sashing units and 12 blocks together to make a vertical row as shown. The row should measure 74½" long. Make a total of six rows.

2 Sew the rows and gray 74½"-long strips together to complete the quilt top.

Finishing the Quilt

Go to ShopMartingale.com/HowtoQuilt if you need more information on finishing techniques.

1 Layer and baste your quilt, and quilt as desired.

2 Using the pink 2¼"-wide strips, prepare and attach the binding.

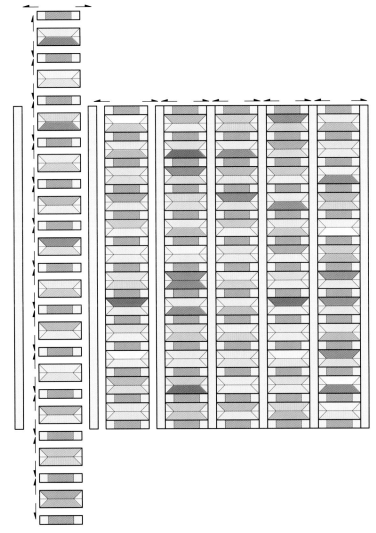

Quilt assembly

Merry-Go-Round

Every little bundle of joy will delight in this lively creation. If you've never tried black in a baby quilt, just look at how the black polka-dot print makes these bright fabrics pop—sure to catch Baby's attention!

FINISHED QUILT: 40" × 50" • **FINISHED BLOCK:** 10" × 10"

Designed and pieced by Regina Girard; machine quilted by Karen Burns of Compulsive Quilting

Materials

Yardage is based on 42"-wide fabric.

20 precut strips, 2½" × 42", in assorted bright colors
  for blocks and binding
⅜ yard of multicolored stripe for blocks
1⅛ yards of black polka dot for block sashing
2 yards of fabric for backing
46" × 56" piece of batting

Cutting

From *each* of the 20 bright strips, cut:

4 squares, 2½" × 2½" (80 total)*
4 rectangles, 2½" × 4½" (80 total)*
Save leftover ends of strips for scrappy binding.

From the multicolored stripe, cut:

4 strips, 2½" × 42"; crosscut into 60 squares, 2½" × 2½"

From the black polka dot, cut:

13 strips, 2½" × 42"; crosscut into:
  40 squares, 2½" × 2½"
  80 rectangles, 2½" × 4½"

*Keep like fabrics together.

Making the Blocks

You'll use pieces from the same bright fabric to make each block, constructing a total of 20 blocks from individual units A, B, and C as described. Press the seam allowances as indicated by the arrows, or as otherwise instructed.

1. For unit A, sew one bright 2½" square to one black polka-dot 2½" square. (Regina recommends that you resist the urge to press the seam allowances toward the black fabric; pressing them open, as indicated by the arrows, will help you align the block seams more accurately later.) Make two matching units for each block (40 total).

2. Sew a matching bright 2½" × 4½" rectangle to each unit from step 1 as shown. Make two matching A units for each block.

Unit A.
Make 2 matching units
for each block.

3. For unit B, sew one bright 2½" square to one striped 2½" square. Be careful to orient the stripes parallel to the seam. Make two matching units for each block (40 total).

4. Sew a matching 2½" × 4½" rectangle to each unit from step 3 as shown. Make two matching B units for each block.

Unit B.
Make 2 matching units
for each block.

REGINA'S TIP FOR UPRIGHT HEARTS

While stripes are inherently directional, some designs include an extra motif that requires a specific orientation (such as the sweet little hearts in the stripe Regina chose). If this is the case with your fabric, you'll need to make one of each of the following units for each block instead of two of unit B as shown in step 4. Pay close attention that you place these units correctly when assembling the blocks so the directional print goes in the same direction throughout.

5 For unit C, sew one striped 2½" square between two black 2½" × 4½" rectangles as shown. Make one unit C for each block (20 total).

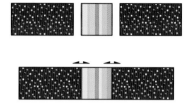

Unit C.
Make 1 for each block.

6 Sew one black 2½" × 4½" rectangle between a matching unit A and unit B as shown. Make two for each block.

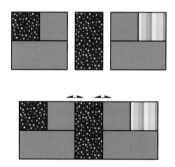

Make 2 for each block.

7 Sew one unit C between the two units made in step 6. Pin the seam intersections carefully. When sewing unit C to each block piece, try sewing with unit C on the bottom. This may make it easier to align the seams. Make 20 blocks.

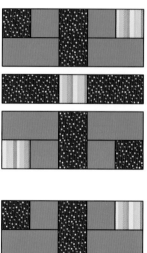

Make 20.

Assembling the Quilt Top

1 Lay out five rows of four blocks each.

2 Pin seam intersections carefully and sew the blocks together into rows; press. Sew the rows together and press the seam allowances in one direction.

Finishing the Quilt

Go to ShopMartingale.com/HowtoQuilt if you need more information on finishing techniques.

1. Layer and baste your quilt, and quilt as desired.

2. Using the leftovers of your bright 2½"-wide strips, prepare and attach the binding.

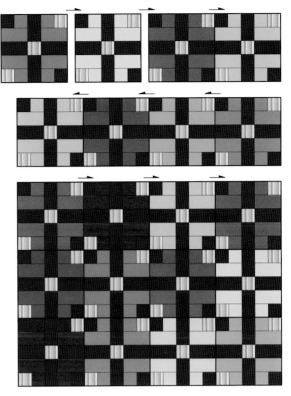

Quilt layout

MONKEY BARS

It's amazing how different a quilt can look with just a change of background fabric. After purchasing a roll of 40 precuts for the Merry-Go-Round quilt and discovering that she had half of the strips left over, designer Regina Girard reached for some different sashing and cornerstone fabrics and made a second project that is equally delightful. If you find yourself in a similar situation with leftover strips, this is a great opportunity to make a baby quilt to donate. Many quilt guilds and charity organizations gather quilts to give to children in need, and often you don't need to finish the quilt top; they'll do it for you. Check with your local quilt guild, quilt shop, or Project Linus (www.projectlinus.org) to learn how you can help or donate a quilt.

FINISHED QUILT: 40½" × 50½"
FINISHED BLOCK: 10" × 10"

Designed and pieced by Regina Girard; machine quilted by Karen Burns of Compulsive Quilting

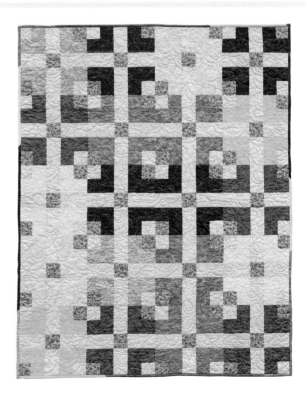

I Love Recess!

Sometimes picking out all of the fabrics for a quilt feels like playtime—while at other times, it's fun to leave that job to somebody else. Whether you mix and match from your stash or opt for beautifully coordinated precuts, this design will show off your strips to perfection.

FINISHED QUILT: 66" × 66" • **FINISHED BLOCK:** 18" × 18"

Designed and pieced by Sara Diepersloot; quilted by Deborah Rasmussen

Materials

Yardage is based on 42"-wide fabric.

36 precut strips, 2½" × 42", of assorted prints for blocks

⅔ yard of muslin for blocks

⅜ yard of green print for inner border

1⅛ yards of blue-and-orange floral for outer border

⅝ yard of fabric for binding

4¼ yards of fabric for backing

72" × 72" piece of batting

Cutting

From *each* of the 36 print strips, cut:

1 rectangle, 2½" × 4½" (36 total)

1 rectangle, 2½" × 6½" (36 total)

1 rectangle, 2½" × 10½" (36 total)

1 rectangle, 2½" × 14½" (36 total)

From the muslin, cut:

8 strips, 2½" × 42"; crosscut into 117 squares, 2½" × 2½"

From the green print, cut:

6 strips, 1¾" × 42"

From the blue-and-orange floral, cut:

7 strips, 5" × 42"

From the binding fabric, cut:

7 strips, 2¼" × 42"

Making the Blocks

Although this is a scrappy quilt, you may wish to use a design wall throughout the assembly process to make sure the fabrics are distributed evenly throughout. The blocks are assembled from the center outward, counterclockwise in rounds using a partial seam. Press the seam allowances as indicated by the arrows, or as otherwise instructed.

1 Layer a muslin square and a print 2½" × 4½" rectangle right sides together as shown. Sew until you are approximately 1" from the bottom edge of the muslin square. Leave the rest of the seam unsewn. You will finish the seam when you sew the last piece of each round. Finger-press the seam allowances away from the muslin.

2 Join a print 2½" × 4½" rectangle to the top edge of the unit from step 1.

3 Join a print 2½" × 4½" rectangle to the left side of the unit.

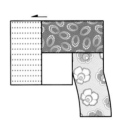

4 Join a print 2½" × 4½" rectangle to the bottom edge of the unit, folding the first rectangle back out of the way.

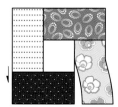

5 Sew the remainder of the seam that was left unsewn in step 1.

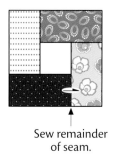

Sew remainder
of seam.

6 Sew muslin squares to one end of *all* the print 2½" × 6½", 2½" × 10½", and 2½" × 14½" rectangles.

7 Add the next round, using the 2½" × 6½" rectangles with muslin squares from step 6. Repeat steps 1–5, leaving the first seam partially unsewn as you did before.

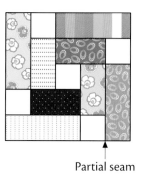

Partial seam

8 Add the next round in the same manner, using the 2½" × 10½" rectangles with muslin squares from step 6. Remember to leave the first seam partially unsewn.

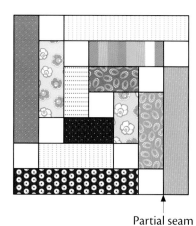

Partial seam

9 Add the last round, using the 2½" × 14½" rectangles with muslin squares from step 6; remember to leave the first seam partially unsewn. Make a total of nine blocks.

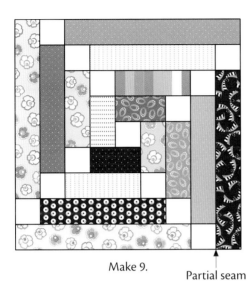

Make 9.

Partial seam

Assembling the Quilt Top

1 Lay out three rows of three blocks each.

2 Sew the blocks together into rows, pressing the seam allowances in opposite directions from row to row. Sew the rows together and press the seam allowances in one direction.

3 Join the green 1¾"-wide strips end to end. Measure the length of the quilt top through the center. Cut two strips to that measurement and sew them to the sides of the quilt top. Measure the width of the quilt top through the center, including the side borders just added. Cut two strips to that measurement and sew them to the top and bottom of the quilt top to complete the inner border.

4 Repeat with the floral 5"-wide strips to add the outer border.

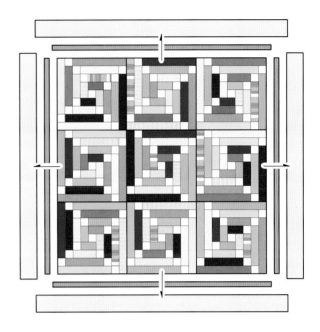

Finishing the Quilt

Go to ShopMartingale.com/HowtoQuilt if you need more information on finishing techniques.

1 Layer and baste your quilt, and quilt as desired.

2 Using the 2¼"-wide binding strips, prepare and attach the binding.

Magic Carpet

Magic Carpet, also known as Many Trips around the World, is the perfect pattern for these romantic pastel fabrics. Divide your strips into six color groups for quick piecing. If you don't have six different colors, simply use one color twice, as designer Nancy Martin did with the white print.

FINISHED QUILT: 62" × 86" • **FINISHED BLOCK:** 12" × 12"

Designed and pieced by Nancy J. Martin; quilted by Wanda Rains

Materials

Yardage is based on 42"-wide fabric.

72 strips, 2½" × 22", consisting of 18 *each* of pink,
   light green, lavender, and yellow prints for blocks
36 strips, 2½" × 22", of white print for blocks
⅜ yard of lavender print for inner border
1⅝ yards of yellow floral for outer border
⅝ yard of yellow stripe for bias binding
5¼ yards of fabric for backing
70" × 94" piece of batting

Cutting

From the lavender print for inner border, cut:
7 strips, 1½" × 42"

From the yellow floral, cut:
8 strips, 6¼" × 42"

From the yellow stripe, cut:
306" of 2¼"-wide bias strips

Making the Blocks

Press the seam allowances as indicated by the arrows,
or as otherwise instructed.

1 Using the 2½" × 22" strips and following the
   illustrations at right, sew three strip sets in each
   color arrangement to make the units. Cut each
   strip set into 8 segments, 2½" wide, for a total of
   24 segments from each color arrangement.

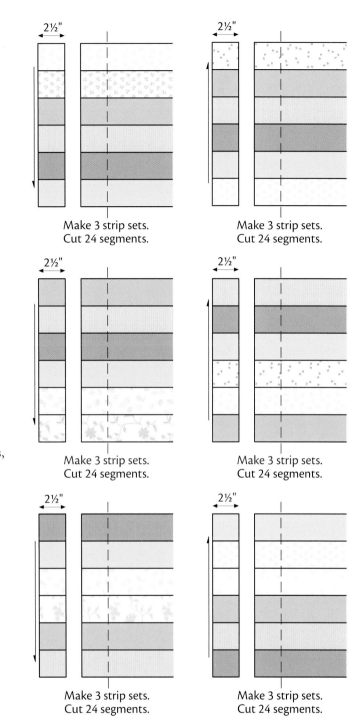

Make 3 strip sets.
Cut 24 segments.

Make 3 strip sets.
Cut 24 segments.

Make 3 strip sets.
Cut 24 segments.

Make 3 strip sets.
Cut 24 segments.

Make 3 strip sets.
Cut 24 segments.

Make 3 strip sets.
Cut 24 segments.

2 Combine one segment from each arrangement as shown to make a block. Make 24 blocks. For ease in joining the blocks, press the seam allowances of 12 blocks in one direction and press in the opposite direction for the other 12 blocks.

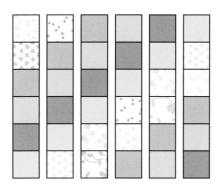

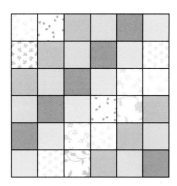

Make 24.

Assembling the Quilt Top

1 Arrange and sew four blocks into a row, rotating the blocks as shown. Make six rows. Press the seam allowances in opposite directions from row to row.

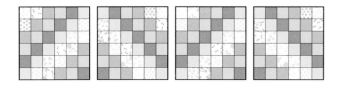

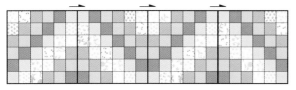

Make 6.

2 Lay out the rows, rotating rows 2, 4, and 6 as shown. Sew the rows together and press the seam allowances in one direction.

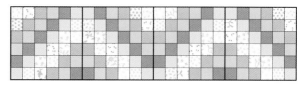

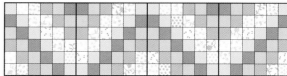

3 Join the lavender 1½"-wide strips end to end. Measure the length of the quilt top through the center. Cut two strips to that measurement and sew them to the sides of the quilt top. Press the seam allowances away from the center. Measure the width of the quilt top through the center, including the borders just added. Cut two strips to that measurement and sew them to the top and bottom of the quilt top to complete the inner border. Press the seam allowances away from the center.

4 Repeat with the yellow floral 6¼"-wide strips to add the outer border.

Finishing the Quilt

Go to ShopMartingale.com/HowtoQuilt if you need more information on finishing techniques.

1 Layer and baste your quilt, and quilt as desired.

2 Using the yellow stripe 2¼"-wide bias strips, prepare and attach the binding.

Adding borders

Nova

The blocks in this quilt appear to be offset, lending movement to the stars. To reproduce the stellar glow, use a variety of batiks in subtle, muted shades.

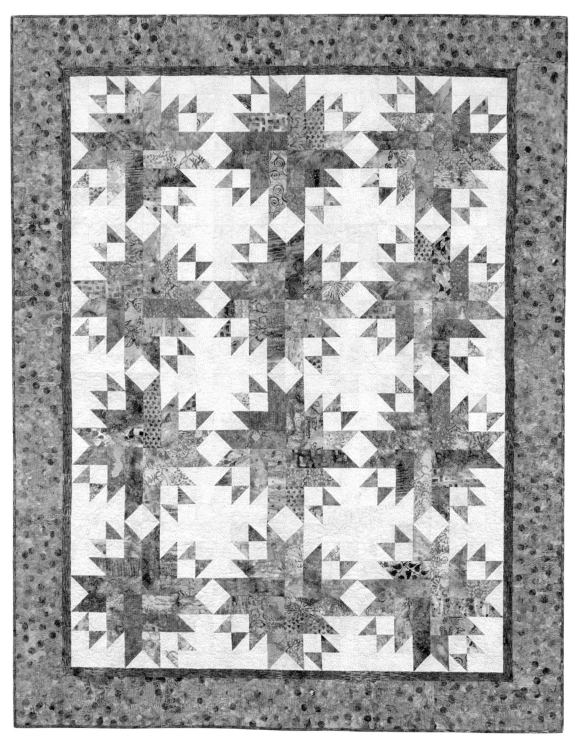

FINISHED QUILT: 61½" × 77½" • **FINISHED BLOCK:** 8" × 8"

Designed and pieced by Kim Brackett; quilted by Karen Williamson

Materials

Yardage is based on 42"-wide fabric.

32 precut strips, 2½" × 42", of assorted dark batiks for blocks

2⅓ yards of light batik for blocks

1 yard of rust batik for inner border and binding

1⅓ yards of multicolored batik for outer border

4¼ yards of fabric for backing

68" × 84" piece of batting

Cutting

From *each* of 16 dark batik strips, cut:

2 rectangles, 2½" × 8½" (32 total)

1 rectangle, 2½" × 6½" (16 total)

1 rectangle, 2½" × 4½" (16 total)

4 squares, 2½" × 2½" (64 total)

From *each* of 16 dark batik strips, cut:

1 rectangle, 2½" × 8½" (16 total)

2 rectangles, 2½" × 6½" (32 total)

2 rectangles, 2½" × 4½" (32 total)

2 squares, 2½" × 2½" (32 total)

From the light batik, cut:

30 strips, 2½" × 42"; crosscut into:

    48 rectangles, 2½" × 6½"

    336 squares, 2½" × 2½"

From the rust batik, cut:

6 strips, 1½" × 42"

8 strips, 2½" × 42"

From the multicolored batik, cut:

7 strips, 6" × 42"

CUTTING FROM YOUR STASH

Time to whittle down your fabric stash? To cut your blocks from scraps rather than using precut 2½" strips as listed in "Materials" at left, follow these instructions.

From assorted dark batiks, cut:

48 rectangles, 2½" × 8½"

48 rectangles, 2½" × 6½"

48 rectangles, 2½" × 4½"

96 squares, 2½" × 2½"

From assorted light batiks, cut:

48 rectangles, 2½" × 6½"

336 squares, 2½" × 2½"

Making the Blocks

Press the seam allowances as indicated by the arrows, or as otherwise instructed.

1. Draw a diagonal line from corner to corner on the wrong side of a light batik 2½" square. Place the marked square on a dark batik 2½" square, right sides together and raw edges aligned. Sew on the line. Trim ¼" from the line on one side and press. Make 96 half-square-triangle units.

Make 96.

2. Sew a light batik 2½" square to a dark side of a half-square-triangle unit as shown. Make 96.

Make 96.

3 Sew together two units from step 2. Carefully clip the seam allowances at the intersection of the units; clip up to, but not through, the stitching. Press the seam allowances in a clockwise direction. Make 48.

Make 48.

4 Referring to the technique used in step 1, place a marked light batik 2½" square on one end of a dark batik 2½" × 4½" rectangle as shown. Stitch, trim, and press. Make 48.

Make 48.

5 Sew a unit from step 4 to a unit from step 3 as shown. Make 48.

Make 48.

6 Referring again to step 1, place a marked light batik 2½" square on one end of a dark batik 2½" × 6½" rectangle as shown. Stitch, trim, and press. Make 48.

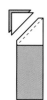

Make 48.

7 Sew a unit from step 6 to a unit from step 5 as shown. Make 48.

Make 48.

8 Sew a light batik 2½" × 6½" rectangle to the top of a unit from step 7. Make 48.

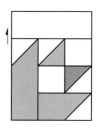

Make 48.

9 Repeating the technique used previously, place a marked light batik 2½" square on one end of a dark batik 2½" × 8½" rectangle. Stitch, trim, and press. Make 48.

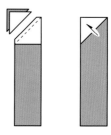

Make 48.

10 Sew a unit from step 9 to a unit from step 8 as shown. Make 48 blocks.

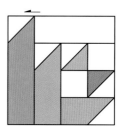

Make 48.

Assembling the Quilt Top

1. Lay out eight rows of six blocks each, orienting the blocks as shown.

2. Sew the blocks together into rows; press. Sew the rows together and press the seam allowances in one direction.

3. Join the rust batik 1½"-wide strips end to end. Measure the length of the quilt top through the center. Cut two strips to that measurement and sew them to the sides of the quilt top. Press the seam allowances away from the center. Measure the width of the quilt top through the center, including the side borders just added. Cut two strips to that measurement and sew them to the top and bottom of the quilt top to complete the inner border. Press the seam allowances away from the center.

4. Repeat with the multicolored batik 6"-wide strips to add the outer border.

Finishing the Quilt

Go to ShopMartingale.com/HowtoQuilt if you need more information on finishing techniques.

1. Layer and baste your quilt, and quilt as desired.

2. Using the rust batik 2½"-wide strips, prepare and attach the binding.

Ocean Waves

These simple blocks suggest a rhythmic wave pattern, but they can be positioned to create many different quilt designs. Once you've made the blocks, try various rotations until you find the arrangement that pleases you most.

FINISHED QUILT: 60" × 60" • **FINISHED BLOCK:** 10" × 10"

Designed, pieced, and quilted by Kate Henderson

Materials

Yardage is based on 42"-wide fabric.

36 precut strips, 2½" × 42", of assorted dark prints for blocks

1¾ yards of cream solid for blocks

⅝ yard of blue solid for binding

3⅞ yards of fabric for backing

66" × 66" piece of batting

Cutting

From *each* of the 36 dark print strips, cut:

1 rectangle, 2½" × 10½" (36 total)

1 rectangle, 2½" × 8½" (36 total)

1 rectangle, 2½" × 6½" (36 total)

1 rectangle, 2½" × 4½" (36 total)

1 square, 2½" × 2½" (36 total)

From the cream solid, cut:

23 strips, 2½" × 42"; crosscut into:

    36 rectangles, 2½" × 8½"

    36 rectangles, 2½" × 6½"

    36 rectangles, 2½" × 4½"

    36 squares, 2½" × 2½"

From the blue solid, cut:

7 strips, 2½" × 42"

Making the Blocks

Press the seam allowances as indicated by the arrows, or as otherwise instructed.

1. Sew a cream 2½" × 8½" rectangle to one side of each print square; a cream 2½" × 6½" rectangle to one end of each print 2½" × 4½" rectangle; a cream 2½" × 4½" rectangle to one end of each print 2½" × 6½" rectangle; and a cream square to one end of each print 2½" × 8½" rectangle.

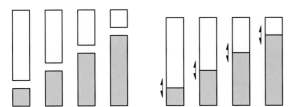

2. Join four pieced units made with a single print and the matching 2½" × 10½" rectangle as shown to make a block. Make 36 blocks.

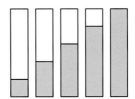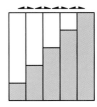

Make 36.

Assembling the Quilt Top

1. Lay out six rows of six blocks each, rotating the blocks as shown or in another layout as desired.

2. Sew the blocks together into rows, and then sew the rows together.

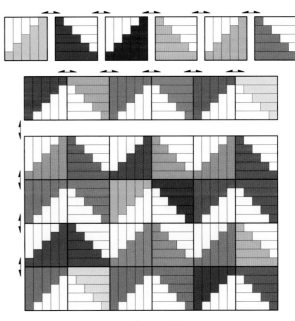

Quilt assembly

Finishing the Quilt

Go to ShopMartingale.com/HowtoQuilt if you need more information on finishing techniques.

1. Layer and baste your quilt, and quilt as desired.

2. Using the blue 2½"-wide strips, prepare and attach the binding.

Cupsicles

Imagine hot, sunny summers of childhood, and paper cups filled with ice and fruity punch for a slushy treat. Now picture mouth-watering fabric shades of fizzy orange, blue raspberry, pineapple yellow, and lemon lime. Thirsty yet?

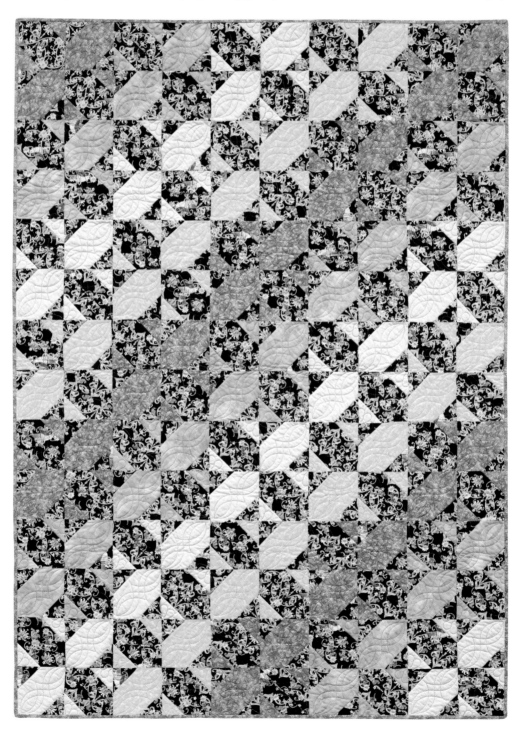

FINISHED QUILT: 55" × 77" • **FINISHED BLOCK:** 11" × 11"

Designed by Kathy Brown; pieced by the Southern Ladies Quilting Society; quilted by Carol Hilton

Materials

Yardage is based on 42"-wide fabric.

1⅔ yards of orange tone on tone for blocks and binding

1 yard *each* of blue, yellow, and green tone on tones for blocks

3¾ yards of black floral for blocks

4¾ yards of fabric for backing

82" × 83" piece of batting

Cutting

From the orange tone on tone, cut:

20 strips, 2½" × 42"

From the blue tone on tone, cut:

12 strips, 2½" × 42"

From the yellow tone on tone, cut:

12 strips, 2½" × 42"

From the green tone on tone, cut:

12 strips, 2½" × 42"

From the black floral, cut:

48 strips, 2½" × 42"

Making the Blocks

Press the seam allowances as indicated by the arrows, or as otherwise instructed.

1 With right sides together, sew a colored strip to a black floral strip. Repeat to make 12 strip sets in each combination.

Make 12.

Make 12.

Make 12.

Make 12.

2 Referring to "Cutting Triangles" on page 9, cut six 90° double-strip triangles from each strip set.

3 Separate the triangles into eight sets of 36 triangles each:
- orange tip/black floral strip
- black floral tip/orange strip
- blue tip/black floral strip
- black floral tip/blue strip
- yellow tip/black floral strip
- black floral tip/yellow strip
- green tip/black floral strip
- black floral tip/green strip

Make 36 of each.

4 With right sides together, sew a black floral tip/orange strip triangle to another black floral tip/orange strip triangle. Repeat to make a total of 18 squares.

Make 18.

5 With right sides together, sew an orange-tip triangle to another orange-tip triangle. Repeat to make a total of 18 squares.

Make 18.

6 From the remaining sets of triangles, make the number of squares indicated below. (You'll have eight triangles left over.) Kathy recommends starching each square to preserve the bias edges of the triangles.

Make 18.   Make 18.

Make 18.   Make 18.

Make 16.   Make 16.

7 With right sides together, join two orange/black squares as shown. Repeat to make a second unit. Join the units to make a block. Repeat to make nine blocks.

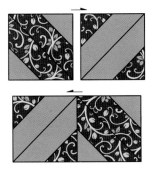

Make 9.

8 Repeat to make nine blue/black blocks, nine yellow/black blocks, and eight green/black blocks.

Assembling the Quilt Top

1 Lay out seven rows of five blocks each as shown, orienting each block so that the black floral strips flow from the upper-left to the lower-right corner of the quilt top, and the colored strips flow from the lower-left to the upper-right corner.

2 Sew the blocks together into rows; press. Sew the rows together and press the seam allowances in one direction. To stabilize the bias edges of the quilt top, stitch around the perimeter ⅛" from the raw edges.

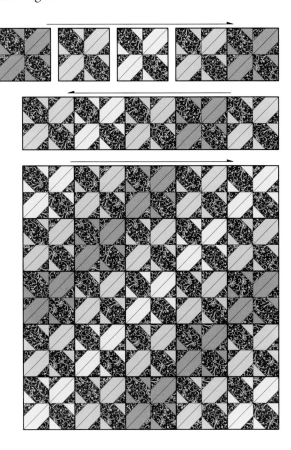

Finishing the Quilt

Go to ShopMartingale.com/HowtoQuilt if you need more information on finishing techniques.

1 Layer and baste your quilt, and quilt as desired.

2 Using the remaining orange 2½"-wide strips, prepare and attach the binding.

Spinners

Imagine rows of pinwheels spinning busily in the summer breeze. Choose your favorite bright, cheerful strips to bring these Pinwheel blocks and pieced borders to life, and you'll enjoy a hint of summer year-round.

FINISHED QUILT: 52" × 52" • **FINISHED BLOCK:** 8" × 8"

Designed by Adrienne Smitke; pieced and quilted by Judy Smitke

Materials

Yardage is based on 42"-wide fabric.

26 precut strips, 2½" × 42", of assorted bright prints for blocks and pieced border

1¼ yards of white-on-white print for block backgrounds

1½ yards of teal print for blocks, border, and binding

3⅜ yards of fabric for backing

58" × 58" piece of batting

Cutting

From the 26 print strips, cut a *total* of:

25 sets of 4 matching rectangles, 2½" × 4½" (100 total)

88 additional assorted rectangles, 2½" × 4½"

From the white-on-white print, cut:

7 strips, 4½" × 42"; crosscut into 100 rectangles, 2½" × 4½"

7 strips, 2½" × 42"; crosscut into 100 squares, 2½" × 2½"

From the teal print, cut:

20 strips, 2½" × 42; crosscut *9 strips* into 144 squares, 2½" × 2½"

Making the Blocks

Each of the 25 blocks is made from four matching bright print rectangles. Press the seam allowances as indicated by the arrows, or as otherwise instructed.

1. Draw a diagonal line from corner to corner on the wrong side of a teal 2½" square. Place the marked square on one end of a white 2½" × 4½" rectangle, right sides together and corners aligned. Sew on the line. Trim the excess corner fabric, leaving a ¼" seam allowance, and press. Make four units for each block (100 total).

Make 100.

2. Repeating the technique used in step 1, place a marked white 2½" square on one end of a bright 2½" × 4½" rectangle as shown. Stitch, trim, and press. Make four matching units.

Make 4.

3. Stitch a unit from step 1 to a unit from step 2 as shown. Repeat with each unit from step 2. Press. You'll have four matching units.

Make 4 matching units.

4. Sew the four units from step 3 into a Pinwheel block as shown.

5. Repeat steps 2–4 to make 25 assorted Pinwheel blocks.

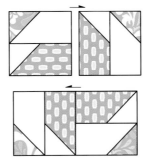 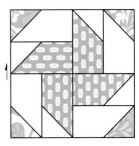

Make 25 with assorted pinwheel colors.

Assembling the Quilt Top

1 Lay out five rows of five blocks each.

2 Sew the blocks together into rows; press. Sew the rows together and press the seam allowances in one direction.

3 Referring to the technique used in step 1 of "Making the Blocks" on page 175, place a marked teal 2½" square on one end of a bright 2½" × 4½" rectangle as shown. Stitch, trim, and press. Make 22 assorted units with the triangle on the right and 22 assorted units with the triangle on the left.

Make 22.

Make 22.

4 Sew a right-side-triangle unit and left-side-triangle unit together so that the teal corner triangles match. Make 20 triangle border blocks. (You'll have four units remaining.)

Make 20.

5 Sew the remaining bright 2½" × 4½" rectangles into pairs to make 20 plain border blocks. (You'll have four rectangles remaining.)

Make 20.

6 Sew two of the remaining units from step 4, four triangle border blocks, and five plain border blocks together as shown. Make two for the side borders.

Side border.
Make 2.

7 Sew two of the remaining 2½" × 4½" rectangles from step 5, six triangle border blocks, and five plain border blocks together as shown. Make two for the top and bottom borders.

Top/bottom border.
Make 2.

8 Sew the pieced side borders to the quilt top, orienting the border strips so that the seams of the teal triangles are aligned with the seams of the teal triangles in the Pinwheel blocks. Sew the pieced top and bottom borders to the quilt top in the same manner.

9 Sew six teal 2½"-wide strips together end to end. Cut two strips, 48½" long, and two strips, 52½" long. Sew the 48½"-long strips to the sides of the quilt top, and sew the 52½"-long strips to the top and bottom.

Finishing the Quilt

Go to ShopMartingale.com/HowtoQuilt if you need more information on finishing techniques.

1 Layer and baste your quilt, and quilt as desired.

2 Using the remaining teal 2½"-wide strips, prepare and attach the binding.

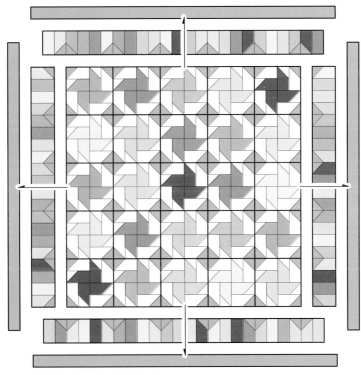

Quilt assembly

Beachside Bungalow

Tropical-fruit colors and prints, combined with perky plaids and stripes, practically beg to adorn a cute seaside cabin. When set against the dark background fabric, the seemingly intertwined rings of color really shine.

FINISHED QUILT: 57" × 68½" • **FINISHED BLOCK:** 8" × 8"

Designed and pieced by Kim Brackett; quilted by Nancy Troyer

Materials

Yardage is based on 42"-wide fabric.
23 precut strips, 2½" × 42", of assorted prints for blocks
2½ yards of charcoal solid for blocks
⅞ yard of white-and-red print for setting triangles
⅝ yard of red print for binding
4 yards of fabric for backing
63" × 73" piece of batting

Cutting

From *each* of 10 print strips, cut:
5 rectangles, 2½" × 4½" (50 total)
6 squares, 2½" × 2½" (60 total)

From *each* of 13 print strips, cut:
4 rectangles, 2½" × 4½" (52 total; 4 are extra)
8 squares, 2½" × 2½" (104 total; 4 are extra)

From the charcoal solid, cut:
13 strips, 4½" × 42"; crosscut into 98 squares,
    4½" × 4½"
9 strips, 2½" × 42"; crosscut into:
    36 rectangles, 2½" × 4½"
    62 squares, 2½" × 2½"

From the white-and-red print, cut:
2 strips, 12⅝" × 42"; crosscut into 6 squares,
    12⅝" × 12⅝". Cut the squares into quarters
    diagonally to yield 24 triangles (2 are extra).

From the red print, cut:
7 strips, 2½" × 42"

CUTTING FROM YOUR STASH

To cut your blocks from scraps rather than using precut 2½" strips as listed in "Materials" above, follow these instructions.

From assorted main prints, cut:
98 rectangles, 2½" × 4½"
160 squares, 2½" × 2½"

From assorted background prints, cut:
98 squares, 4½" × 4½"
36 rectangles, 2½" × 4½"
62 squares, 2½" × 2½"

Making the Blocks

Press the seam allowances as indicated by the arrows, or as otherwise instructed.

1   Draw a diagonal line from corner to corner on the wrong side of a print 2½" square. Place the marked square on one corner of a charcoal 4½" square, right sides together and corners aligned. Sew on the line. Trim the excess corner fabric, leaving a ¼" seam allowance, and press. Make 98.

Make 98.

2   Sew a print 2½" × 4½" rectangle to a charcoal 2½" × 4½" rectangle. Make 36. Press 18 units toward the charcoal rectangle and 18 toward the print rectangle.

Make 18.   Make 18.

3   To make block A, select two units from step 1 and one of each unit from step 2. For the rectangle unit on top, choose a unit with seam allowances pressed toward the print fabric. For the bottom rectangle unit, choose a unit with seam allowances pressed toward the charcoal fabric.

4 Sew the units together to make block A as shown. Make a total of 18.

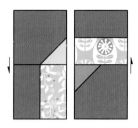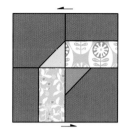

Block A.
Make 18.

5 Sew a charcoal 2½" square to a print 2½" square. Make 62.

Make 62.

6 Sew a print 2½" × 4½" rectangle to each unit from step 5 as shown. Make 62.

Make 62.

7 Sew two units from step 6 and two units from step 1 together as shown to make block B. Carefully clip the seam allowances at the intersection of the units; clip up to, but not through, the stitching. Press the seam allowances in a counterclockwise direction. Make a total of 31.

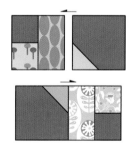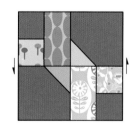

Block B.
Make 31.

Assembling the Quilt Top

1 Arrange the blocks and white-and-red setting triangles in diagonal rows as shown, placing the A blocks around the outside edges and the B blocks in the center.

2 Sew the blocks together into rows; press. Sew the rows together and press the seam allowances in one direction.

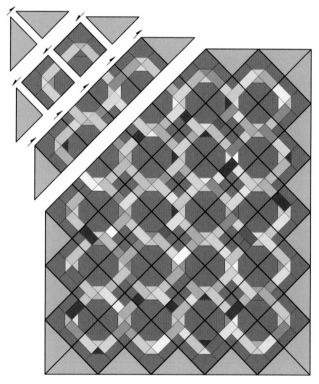

Quilt assembly

Finishing the Quilt

Go to ShopMartingale.com/HowtoQuilt if you need more information on finishing techniques.

1 Layer and baste your quilt, and quilt as desired.

2 Using the red 2½"-wide strips, prepare and attach the binding.

Flower Boxes

The arrangement of this quilt center creates an illusion of layered blocks. If you aren't particularly fond of pastels, replace them with dark prints and swap in a light background fabric instead of the dark brown.

FINISHED QUILT: 64½" × 64½" • **FINISHED BLOCK:** 8" × 8"

Designed by Kim Brackett; pieced and quilted by Karen Williamson

Materials

Yardage is based on 42"-wide fabric.

64 precut strips, 2½" × 42", of assorted pastel prints for blocks

2⅜ yards of brown marbled print for blocks and binding

4½ yards of fabric for backing

68½" × 68½" piece of batting

Cutting

From *each* of the 64 pastel print strips, cut:

1 rectangle, 2½" × 8½" (64 total)

2 rectangles, 2½" × 6½" (128 total)

2 rectangles, 2½" × 4½" (128 total)

1 square, 2½" × 2½" (64 total)

From the brown marbled print, cut:

31 strips, 2½" × 42"; crosscut *24 strips* into 384 squares, 2½" × 2½"

CUTTING FROM YOUR STASH

Time to whittle down your fabric stash? To cut your blocks from scraps rather than using precut 2½" strips as listed in "Materials" above, follow these instructions.

From assorted pastel prints, cut:

64 rectangles, 2½" × 8½"

128 rectangles, 2½" × 6½"

128 rectangles, 2½" × 4½"

64 squares, 2½" × 2½"

From assorted dark brown prints, cut:

384 squares, 2½" × 2½"

Making the Blocks

Press the seam allowances as indicated by the arrows, or as otherwise instructed.

1 Draw a diagonal line from corner to corner on the wrong side of a pastel 2½" square. Place the marked square on a brown 2½" square, right sides together and raw edges aligned. Sew on the line. Trim ¼" from the line on one side and press. Make 64.

Make 64.

2 Sew a brown 2½" square to a light side of a half-square-triangle unit as shown. Make 64.

Make 64.

3 Referring to the technique used in step 1, place a marked brown 2½" square on one end of a pastel 2½" × 4½" rectangle as shown. Stitch, trim, and press. Make 128.

Make 128.

4 Sew together one unit from step 2 and two units from step 3 as shown. Make 64.

     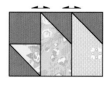

Make 64.

5 Referring again to the technique in step 1, place two marked brown 2½" squares on opposite ends of a pastel 2½" × 6½" rectangle as shown. Stitch, trim, and press. Make 64.

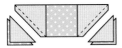 

Make 64.

6 Sew a unit from step 5 to the bottom of a unit from step 4 as shown. Make 64.

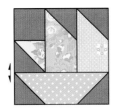

Make 64.

7 Sew a pastel 2½" × 6½" rectangle to the top of a unit from step 6. Make 64.

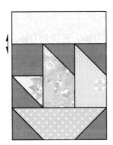

Make 64.

8 Sew a pastel 2½" × 8½" rectangle to one side of a unit from step 7 as shown. Make 64 blocks.

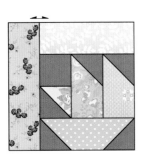

Make 64.

Assembling the Quilt Top

1 Lay out eight rows of eight blocks each, orienting the blocks as shown.

2 Sew the blocks together into rows; press. Join the rows and press the seam allowances open.

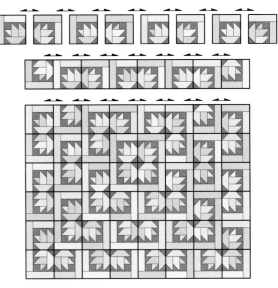

Quilt assembly

Finishing the Quilt

Go to ShopMartingale.com/HowtoQuilt if you need more information on finishing techniques.

1 Layer and baste your quilt, and quilt as desired.

2 Using the remaining brown 2½"-wide strips, prepare and attach the binding.

Pastelmania

These soft pastels bring to mind sunny days and warm breezes.
The interplay of strip-set squares and pieced setting triangles
invites you to take a closer look at this quick and easy design.

FINISHED QUILT: 61¾" × 84½" • **FINISHED BLOCK:** 8" × 8"

Designed, pieced, and quilted by Cheryl Brown

Materials

Yardage is based on 42"-wide fabric. Fat quarters measure 18" × 21".

40 precut strips, 2½" × 42", of assorted pastel batiks for blocks and pieced second border

1⅞ yards of blue tone-on-tone batik for pieced setting triangles, first and third borders, and bias binding

6 or 7 fat quarters of assorted pastel batiks for setting squares and pieced setting triangles

1 yard of pastel batik for fourth border

5 yards of fabric for backing

68" × 91" piece of batting

Cutting

From the blue tone-on-tone batik, cut:

13 strips, 1½" × 42"

7 strips, 2" × 42"; crosscut into:
    16 rectangles, 2" × 12⅝"
    4 rectangles, 2" × 5⅛"
    4 rectangles, 2" × 6⅝"

310" of 2¼"-wide bias strips

From the pastel fat quarters, cut a *total* of:

9 squares, 8½" × 8½"

4 squares, 9⅝" × 9⅝"; cut the squares into quarters diagonally to yield 16 triangles

2 squares, 3⅝" × 3⅝"; cut the squares in half diagonally to yield 4 triangles

From the pastel batik for 4th border, cut:

7 strips, 4½" × 42"

Making the Blocks and Setting Triangles

Press the seam allowances as indicated by the arrows, or as otherwise instructed.

1. Randomly select four pastel 2½" × 42" strips and sew them together along the long edges to make a strip set. Make 10. Crosscut each strip set into three squares, 8½" wide, for blocks, and three segments, 2½" wide. Cut one extra 2½"-wide segment from one strip set. Set the 2½" segments aside for the pieced border.

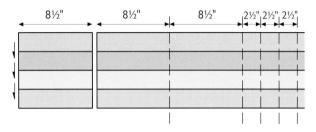

Make 10 strip sets.
Cut 30 squares. Cut 31 border units.

2. Trim each blue 2" × 12⅝" rectangle on both ends at a 45° angle from the bottom corners as shown. Sew a trimmed rectangle to the long edge of each pastel quarter-square triangle, offsetting the corners as shown. Make 16.

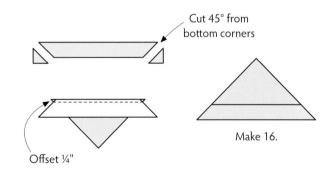

Cut 45° from bottom corners

Offset ¼"

Make 16.

3. Trim each blue 2" × 5⅛" rectangle on one end at a 45° angle from the corner as shown. Sew to the left side of each pastel half-square triangle as shown. Make four.

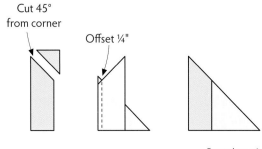

Cut 45° from corner

Offset ¼"

4 Trim each blue 2" × 6⅝" rectangle on one end at a 45° angle from the corner as shown. Sew to the bottom of each pastel half-square-triangle unit as shown. Make four.

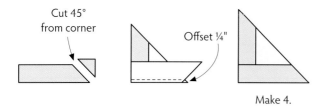

Cut 45° from corner

Offset ¼"

Make 4.

Assembling the Quilt Top

1 Arrange the pieced blocks, the pastel 8½" squares, and the pieced setting triangles in diagonal rows as shown in the quilt diagram at right. Note the differing orientation of the pieced blocks within each diagonal row.

2 Sew the pieces together into diagonal rows. Press the seam allowances toward the sides without seams. Sew the rows together, adding the corner triangles last; press.

3 Join six of the blue 1½"-wide strips end to end. Measure the width of the quilt top through the center and cut two strips to that measurement. Sew the strips to the top and bottom of the quilt top and press the seam allowances toward the border. Measure the length of the quilt top through the center, including the borders just added. Cut two strips to that measurement and sew them to the sides of the quilt top to complete the first border.

4 Join the 2½"-wide strip-set segments end to end. Repeat step 3 to add the second border.

5 Repeat with the remaining blue 1½"-wide strips to add the third border.

6 Repeat with the pastel 4½"-wide strips to add the fourth border.

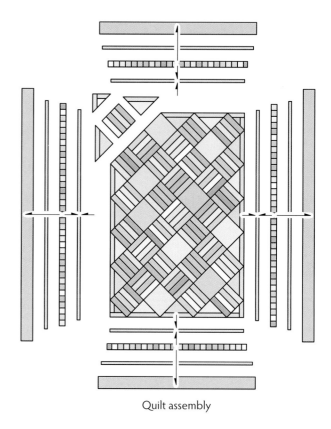

Quilt assembly

Finishing the Quilt

Go to ShopMartingale.com/HowtoQuilt if you need more information on finishing techniques.

1 Layer and baste your quilt, and quilt as desired.

2 Using the blue 2¼"-wide bias strips, prepare and attach the binding.

Snail Takes a Detour

This Snail's Trail variation relies on strong contrast between the light and dark fabrics to enhance the design. Have some fun choosing an unexpected print motif for the wide outer border.

FINISHED QUILT: 71½" × 71½" • **FINISHED BLOCK:** 8" × 8"

Designed, pieced, and quilted by Kim Brackett

Materials

Yardage is based on 42"-wide fabric.

32 precut strips, 2½" × 42", of assorted dark prints in green, burgundy, and brown for blocks

32 precut strips, 2½" × 42", of assorted light tan prints for blocks

⅜ yard of brown print for inner border

2 yards of novelty print for outer border and binding

5 yards of fabric for backing

78" × 78" piece of batting

Cutting

From *each* of 17 dark print and 17 light print strips, cut:

2 rectangles, 2½" × 5½" (34 dark and 34 light total)

5 rectangles, 2½" × 4½" (85 dark and 85 light total)*

2 squares, 2½" × 2½" (34 dark and 34 light total)**

From *each* of 13 dark print and 13 light print strips, cut:

2 rectangles, 2½" × 5½" (26 dark and 26 light total)

4 rectangles, 2½" × 4½" (52 dark and 52 light total)*

3 squares, 2½" × 2½" (39 dark and 39 light total)**

From *each* of 2 dark print and 2 light print strips, cut:

4 rectangles, 2½" × 4½" (8 dark and 8 light total)*

6 squares, 2½" × 2½" (12 dark and 12 light total)**

From the brown print, cut:

7 strips, 1½" × 42"

From the novelty print, cut:

7 strips, 6" × 42"

8 strips, 2½" × 42"

There will be a total of 145 dark and 145 light 2½" × 4½" rectangles; you will have 1 dark and 1 light rectangle left over.

**There will be a total of 85 dark and 85 light 2½" squares; you will have 1 dark square left over.*

Time to whittle down your fabric stash? To cut your blocks from scraps rather than using precut 2½" strips as listed in "Materials" at left, follow these instructions.

From dark print scraps, cut:

60 rectangles, 2½" × 5½"

144 rectangles, 2½" × 4½"

84 squares, 2½" × 2½"

From light print scraps, cut:

60 rectangles, 2½" × 5½"

144 rectangles, 2½" × 4½"

85 squares, 2½" × 2½"

Making the Blocks and Sashing Units

Press the seam allowances as indicated by the arrows, or as otherwise instructed.

1 Draw a diagonal line from corner to corner on the wrong side of a dark 2½" square. Place the marked square on one end of a light 2½" × 4½" rectangle, right sides together and corners aligned. Sew on the line. Trim the excess corner fabric, leaving a ¼" seam allowance, and press. Make 72 of these light units. Repeat with the light 2½" squares and dark 2½" × 4½" rectangles, keeping the seam angle the same. Make 72 of these dark units.

Light folded-corner unit. Make 72.

Dark folded-corner unit. Make 72.

2 Sew a dark 2½" × 4½" rectangle to each light unit and sew a light 2½" × 4½" rectangle to each dark unit as shown. Make 72 of each, 144 total.

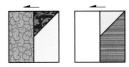

Make 72 of each.

3 Join two of each of the two units from step 2 as shown to complete one block. Carefully clip the seam allowances at the intersection of the units; clip up to, but not through, the stitching. Press the seam allowances in a counterclockwise direction. Make 36 blocks.

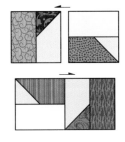 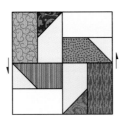

Make 36.

4 Place a light 2½" × 5½" rectangle at right angles on a dark 2½" × 5½" rectangle, right sides together and corners aligned. Draw a diagonal line on the light rectangle as shown. Sew on the line. Trim the corner fabric, leaving a ¼" seam allowance, and press. Make 60 sashing units.

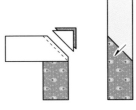

Make 60.

Assembling the Quilt Top

1 Arrange the blocks, sashing units, and light and dark squares as shown above right.

2 Sew the pieces together into rows; press. Sew the rows together and press the seam allowances in one direction.

3 Join the brown 1½"-wide strips end to end. Measure the length of the quilt top through the center. Cut two strips to that measurement and sew them to the sides of the quilt top. Press the seam allowances away from the center. Measure the width of the quilt top through the center, including the side borders just added. Cut two strips to that measurement and sew them to the top and bottom of the quilt top to complete the inner border. Press the seam allowances away from the center.

4 Repeat with the novelty print 6"-wide strips to add the outer border.

Finishing the Quilt

Go to ShopMartingale.com/HowtoQuilt if you need more information on finishing techniques.

1 Layer and baste your quilt, and quilt as desired.

2 Using the novelty print 2½"-wide strips, prepare and attach the binding.

Razzmatazz

Prominent shapes in a jazzy color palette create a feast for the eyes.
Choose strips and squares of primarily medium and dark prints,
adding just enough light cream to the composition for contrast.

FINISHED QUILT: 44" × 60" • **FINISHED BLOCK:** 8" × 8"

Designed, pieced, and quilted by Stan Green

Materials

Yardage is based on 42"-wide fabric.

24 precut strips, 2½" × 42", of assorted medium to dark rich-toned prints for blocks and inner border

5 precut strips, 2½" × 42", of assorted light prints for blocks and inner border

7 squares, 10" × 10", of assorted medium to dark prints for blocks and border squares

6 squares, 10" × 10", of assorted light prints for blocks and border squares

⅝ yard of dark red print for outer border

½ yard of yellow polka dot for binding

2 yards of fabric for backing

50" × 68" piece of batting

Cutting

From *each* of 6 dark print strips, cut:
8 squares, 2½" × 2½" (48 total)*

From *each* of 6 medium print strips, cut:
8 squares, 2½" × 2½" (48 total)*

From *each* of 6 medium or dark print strips, cut:
8 rectangles, 2½" × 4½" (48 total)*

From *each* of 6 different medium or dark print strips, cut:
8 squares, 2½" × 2½" (48 total)*

From the assorted light strips, cut a *total* of:
6 strips, 2½" × 16½"
4 strips, 2½" × 18½"

From *each* of 6 light print squares, cut:
8 squares, 2⅞" × 2⅞" (48 total); cut the squares in half diagonally to yield 96 triangles*

From *each* of 6 medium or dark print squares, cut:
4 squares, 4⅞" × 4⅞" (24 total); cut the squares in half diagonally to yield 48 triangles*

From 1 medium or dark print square, cut:
4 squares, 4½" × 4½"

From the dark red print, cut:
5 strips, 4½" × 42"

From the yellow polka dot, cut:
6 strips, 2½" × 42"

*Keep like fabrics together.

CUTTING FROM YOUR STASH

Time to whittle down your fabric stash? To cut your blocks from scraps rather than using precut 2½" strips as listed in "Materials" at left, follow these instructions.

¼ yard *each* of 6 cream prints

¼ yard or 1 fat eighth (9" × 21") *each* of 6 medium to dark prints

10 strips, 2½" × 42", of assorted medium to dark prints

Making the Blocks

You will construct four matching 8" × 8" blocks and combine them to make a 16" jumbo block. Instructions are given for making one jumbo block at a time. Press the seam allowances as indicated by the arrows, or as otherwise instructed.

1. Sort the cut fabric pieces into six jumbo blocks. Each block needs:
   - 8 matching dark 2½" squares
   - 8 matching medium 2½" squares
   - 8 matching medium or dark 2½" squares that are visually distinct from (don't blend with) the first 2 sets of squares
   - 16 matching light 2⅞" triangles
   - 8 matching 2½" × 4½" rectangles
   - 8 matching 4⅞" triangles

2. Sew two matching medium 2½" squares to two matching dark 2½" squares as shown to make a four-patch unit. Make four units.

Make 4.

3 Sew a light 2⅞" triangle to one end of each 2½" × 4½" rectangle. Make four units with the triangle slanting in one direction and four units with the triangle slanting in the opposite direction. This creates units that look like mirror images of each other. (Do not trim the tips of the triangles extending past the rectangle edge. The tips will be used to help sew the 4⅞" triangles to the corners in step 6.) You'll have eight light triangles remaining for step 4.

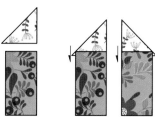

Make 4 of each.

4 Sew a light 2⅞" triangle to each remaining 2½" square. Make four units with the triangle slanting in one direction and four mirror-image units with the triangles slanting in the opposite direction. The tips of the triangles will extend past the square, but do not trim them.

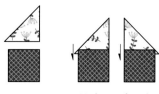

Make 4 of each.

5 Arrange one unit from step 2 and two mirror-image units each from steps 3 and 4 as shown. Sew the units together and press as indicated to make the inner part of a block. Make four inner-block units and press.

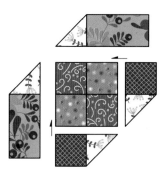

Inner block.
Make 4.

6 Sew a 4⅞" triangle to each unfinished corner of the inner blocks. Use the light triangle tips to position the corner triangles. The tips should line up if your seam allowances are consistent. Make four matching blocks. They should each measure 8½" square.

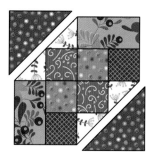

8½" block.
Make 4.

7 Arrange the four blocks from step 6, rotating them so the 2½" × 4½" rectangles butt together to create a nice frame for the finished unit. Sew the blocks together to make one jumbo block.

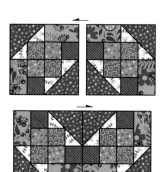

Jumbo block.
Make 1.

8 Repeat steps 2–7 to make five more jumbo blocks, mixing up the colors so that the units stand out from one another. Refer to the photo on page 190 for color examples.

Assembling the Quilt Top

1. Arrange the six jumbo blocks in three rows of two blocks each.

2. Sew the blocks together into rows; press. Sew the rows together and press the seam allowances in one direction.

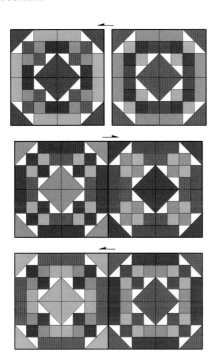

3. Join two light 2½" × 16½" strips end to end and attach this strip to the top of the quilt top. Repeat for the bottom border. For the side border, sew a light 2½" × 18½" strip to each end of a light 2½" × 16½" strip. Make two and join them to the sides of the quilt top to complete the inner border.

4. Trim two dark red 4½" × 42" strips to 37½" long and sew them to the top and bottom of the quilt top. For the outer side borders, join the three remaining dark red 4½" × 42" strips end to end.

From the pieced strip, cut two strips, 52½" long. Sew a medium or dark 4½" square to each end of the strips, and sew the strips to the sides of the quilt top to complete the outer border.

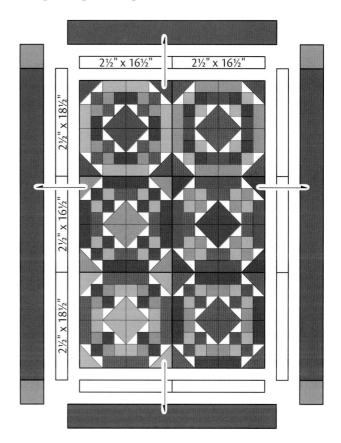

Finishing the Quilt

Go to ShopMartingale.com/HowtoQuilt if you need more information on finishing techniques.

1. Layer and baste your quilt, and quilt as desired.

2. Using the yellow polka-dot 2½"-wide strips, prepare and attach the binding.

Tool Shed

Pieced entirely from random scraps, this quilt shows what can be accomplished by veering away from the safety of a fabric collection. Looking at all the different light and dark fabrics in these blocks may help free you to step outside of your own comfort zone.

FINISHED QUILT: 54½" × 62½" • **FINISHED BLOCK:** 8" × 8"

Designed by Kim Brackett; pieced and quilted by Darlene Johannis

Materials

Yardage is based on 42"-wide fabric.

30 strips, 2½" × at least 31", of assorted dark prints for blocks

30 strips, 2½" × at least 31", of assorted light prints for blocks

⅓ yard of black print for inner border

1¾ yards of red print for outer border and binding

4 yards of fabric for backing

61" × 69" piece of batting

Cutting

From *each* of the 30 dark print strips, cut:

8 rectangles, 2½" × 3½" (240 total)

From *each* of the 30 light print strips, cut:

8 rectangles, 2½" × 3½" (240 total)

From the black print, cut:

5 strips, 1½" × 42"

From the red print, cut:

6 strips, 6½" × 42"

7 strips, 2½" × 42"

CUTTING FROM YOUR STASH

Time to whittle down your fabric stash? To cut your blocks from scraps rather than using precut 2½" strips as listed in "Materials" above, follow these instructions.

From assorted dark prints, cut:

60 sets of 4 rectangles, 2½" × 3½" (240 total)

From assorted light prints, cut:

30 sets of 8 rectangles, 2½" × 3½" (240 total)

Making the Blocks

Press the seam allowances as indicated by the arrows, or as otherwise instructed.

1 Select eight matching light 2½" × 3½" rectangles and two sets of four matching dark 2½" × 3½" rectangles. Place a light rectangle at right angles on a dark rectangle, right sides together and corners aligned. Draw a diagonal line on the light rectangle as shown. Sew on the line. Trim the excess corner fabric, leaving a ¼" seam allowance, and press toward the dark units. Make two sets of four matching units for each of the 30 blocks.

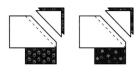

Make 2 sets of 4
for each block.

2 Sew together one of each step 1 unit from each block set as shown. Make four units for each block. Press the seam allowances in the same direction for each set of units.

Make 4
for each block.

3 Sew together the four units from step 2 as shown. Carefully clip the seam allowances at the intersection of the units; clip up to, but not through, the stitching. Press the seam allowances in a clockwise direction. Make 30 blocks.

 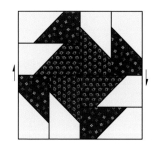

Make 30.

Assembling the Quilt Top

1 Lay out six rows of five blocks each.

2 Sew the blocks together into rows; press. Sew the rows together and press the seam allowances in one direction.

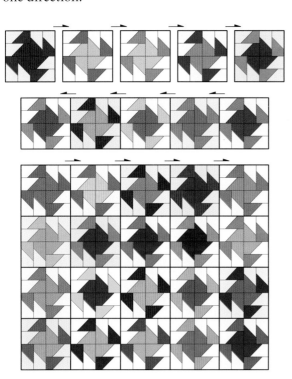

3 Join the black 1½"-wide strips end to end. Measure the length of the quilt top through the center. Cut two strips to that measurement and sew them to the sides of the quilt top. Press the seam allowances away from the center. Measure the width of the quilt top through the center, including the side borders just added. Cut two strips to that measurement and sew them to the top and bottom of the quilt top to complete the inner border. Press the seam allowances away from the center.

4 Repeat with the red 6½"-wide strips to add the outer border.

Finishing the Quilt

Go to ShopMartingale.com/HowtoQuilt if you need more information on finishing techniques.

1 Layer and baste your quilt, and quilt as desired.

2 Using the red 2½"-wide strips, prepare and attach the binding.

Wind Farm

////////////////

Is it any wonder that Pinwheel blocks are ever-popular? Their personality shines in almost any fabric style or layout. Gathered in groups of four and decked out in an adorable array of prints, they look like eclectic little wind farms.

FINISHED QUILT: 54" × 76" • **FINISHED BLOCK:** 20" × 20"

Designed, pieced, and quilted by Kate Henderson

Materials

Yardage is based on 42"-wide fabric. Fat quarters measure 18" × 21".

24 fat quarters of assorted dark prints for blocks, pieced inner border, and binding

2⅜ yards of white solid for blocks, sashing, and borders

4⅝ yards of fabric for backing

60" × 82" piece of batting

Cutting

From *each* of the 24 print fat quarters, cut:

5 strips, 2½" × 21"; crosscut into:

    2 strips, 2½" × 19" (48 total)

    1 strip, 2½" × 12" (24 total)

    6 rectangles, 2½" × 4½" (144 total)

From the remainders of the print fat quarters, cut:

18 assorted squares, 2½" × 2½"

2 rectangles, 2½" × 4½"

From the white solid, cut:

33 strips, 2½" × 42"; crosscut *16 strips* into 256 squares, 2½" × 2½"

Making the Blocks

Press the seam allowances as indicated by the arrows, or as otherwise instructed.

1. Organize the 2½" × 19" strips into pairs. Sew the pairs together into strip sets. Cut each strip set into four squares, 4½" × 4½" (96 total).

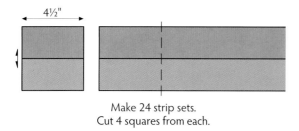

4½"

Make 24 strip sets.
Cut 4 squares from each.

2. Sew together two matching units from step 1 as shown. Make two.

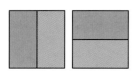 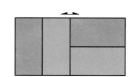

3. Sew together the two units from step 2 as shown. Repeat to make 24 pinwheel units.

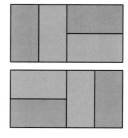 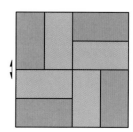

Make 24.

4. Arrange four pinwheel units from step 3 into two rows of two. Sew the units together into rows, press, and then sew the rows together. Repeat to make six block centers.

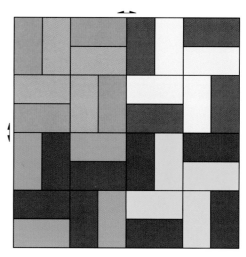

Make 6.

5. Draw a diagonal line from corner to corner on the wrong side of two white 2½" squares. Place a marked square on one end of a print 2½" × 4½" rectangle, right sides together and corners aligned. Sew on the line. Trim the excess corner fabric, leaving a ¼" seam allowance, and press. Repeat on the other end of the rectangle to make a flying-geese unit as shown. Make 96.

Make 96.

6 Sew four flying-geese units together end to end. Make 12 for side units.

Make 12.

7 Sew four flying-geese units together end to end. Sew a white square to each end of the pieced unit. Make 12 for top and bottom units.

Make 12.

8 Sew side units to opposite sides of a block center from step 4, orienting the units as shown. Sew top and bottom units to the block center. Make six.

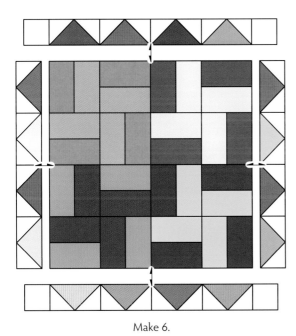

Make 6.

Assembling the Quilt Top

1 From two white strips, cut four 2½" × 20½" sashing strips. Sew three blocks and two white sashing strips together, alternating them as shown. Make two.

2 Join five white strips end to end. From the pieced strip, cut three sashing strips, 64½" long. Join the block columns from step 1 with 64½"-long sashing strips on both sides and in the middle.

3 Join three white strips end to end. From the pieced strip, cut two sashing strips, 46½" long. Sew the strips to the top and bottom of the quilt top.

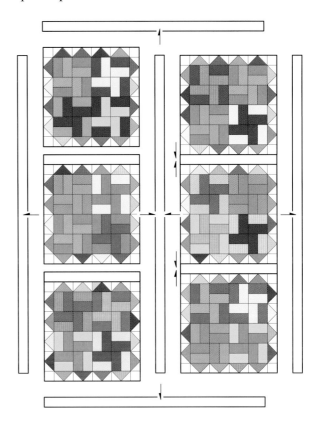

4 Referring to step 5 of "Making the Blocks" on page 198, place a marked white 2½" square on one end of a print 2½" × 4½" rectangle. Stitch, trim, and press. Make 20 of unit A and 20 of unit B.

Unit A.   Unit B.
Make 20.   Make 20.

5 Sew six of unit A, six of unit B, three print 2½" × 4½" rectangles, and four print squares together as shown. Make two for side borders. Referring to the diagram on page 200, sew the pieced borders to the sides of the quilt top.

Make 2.

6 Sew four of unit A, four of unit B, two print 2½" × 4½" rectangles, and five print squares together as shown. Make two for the top and bottom borders. Referring to the quilt diagram, sew the pieced borders to the top and bottom of the quilt top.

Make 2.

7 Join two white strips end to end. Make two. Trim each pieced strip to 72½" long. Join three white strips end to end. From the pieced strip, cut two strips, 54½" long. Sew the 72½"-long strips to the sides of the quilt top, and then sew the 54½"-long strips to the top and bottom to complete the outer border.

Finishing the Quilt

Go to ShopMartingale.com/HowtoQuilt if you need more information on finishing techniques.

1 Layer and baste your quilt, and quilt as desired.

2 Using the print 2½" × 12" strips, prepare and attach the binding.

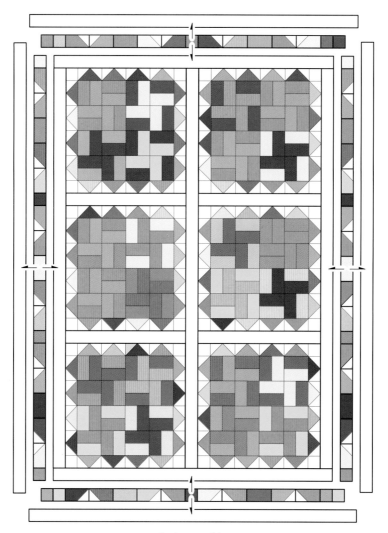

Quilt assembly

Irene's Vexation

////////////////

Don't be deceived by the name—this quilt is a delight to make. Irene is Kim's imaginary "bad self," who sometimes gets peeved over things like doing math for a pieced border. Serenity prevailed, though, and the quilt gained a scrappy border that sparkles.

FINISHED QUILT: 48½" × 60½" • **FINISHED BLOCK:** 12" × 12"

Designed, pieced, and quilted by Kim Brackett

Materials

Yardage is based on 42"-wide fabric.

24 precut strips, 2½" × 42", of assorted dark prints for blocks and pieced outer border

12 *pairs* of precut strips, 2½" × 42", of assorted light prints for blocks and pieced outer border

1 yard of blue floral for inner border and binding

3½ yards of fabric for backing

55" × 67" piece of batting

Cutting

Select 12 assorted dark strips for the short pinwheel "blades" and 12 assorted dark strips for the long pinwheel "blades."

From *each* of the 12 short "blade" strips, cut:

4 rectangles, 2½" × 4½" (48 total)

8 squares, 2½" × 2½" (96 total; 8 are extra)

From *each* of the 12 long "blade" strips, cut:

4 rectangles, 2½" × 6½" (48 total)

5 squares, 2½" × 2½" (60 total)

From *each pair* of assorted light strips, cut:

4 rectangles, 2½" × 6½" (48 total)

17 squares, 2½" × 2½" (204 total; 8 are extra)

From the blue floral, cut:

11 strips, 2½" × 42"

Making the Blocks

Press the seam allowances as indicated by the arrows, or as otherwise instructed.

1 Draw a diagonal line from corner to corner on the wrong side of a light 2½" square. Place the marked square on one end of a dark 2½" × 4½" rectangle, right sides together and corners aligned. Sew on the line. Trim the excess corner fabric, leaving a ¼" seam allowance, and press. Make four matching units.

Make 4.

CUTTING FROM YOUR STASH

Time to whittle down your fabric stash? To cut your blocks from scraps rather than using precut 2½" strips as listed in "Materials" at left, follow these instructions.

From assorted dark prints, cut:

12 sets of 4 rectangles, 2½" × 6½" (48 total)

12 sets of:

4 rectangles, 2½" × 4½" (48 total)

4 squares, 2½" × 2½" (48 total)

From assorted light prints, cut:

12 sets of:

4 rectangles, 2½" × 6½" (48 total)

8 squares, 2½" × 2½" (96 total)

From light scraps, cut:

100 squares, 2½" × 2½"

From dark scraps, cut:

100 squares, 2½" × 2½"

2 Sew a matching light 2½" square to each unit from step 1 as shown.

Make 4.

3 Referring to the technique used in step 1, place a marked 2½" square that matches the dark print from step 2 on one end of a 2½" × 6½" rectangle of a different print. Stitch, trim, and press. Make four matching units.

Make 4.

4 Sew the units from steps 2 and 3 together as shown. Make four units.

Make 4.

5 Sew a matching light 2½" × 6½" rectangle to the top of each unit from step 4.

Make 4.

6 Sew the four units from step 5 together as shown. Carefully clip the seam allowances at the intersection of the units; clip up to, but not through, the stitching. Press the seam allowances in a counterclockwise direction. Make a total of 12 blocks.

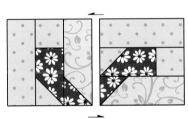

Make 12 blocks.

Assembling the Quilt Top

1 Lay out four rows of three blocks each.

2 Sew the blocks together into rows; press. Sew the rows together and press the seam allowances in one direction.

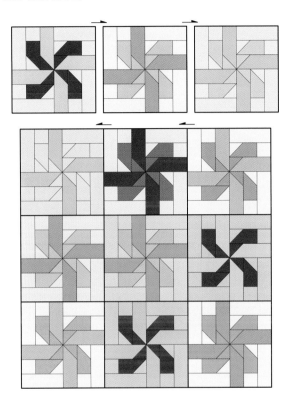

3 Join five of the blue floral 2½"-wide strips end to end. Cut two strips, 48½" long, and two strips, 40½" long. Sew the 48½"-long strips to the sides of the quilt top, and then sew the 40½"-long strips to the top and bottom.

4 From the remaining light and dark 2½" squares, assemble four-patch units for the pieced border as shown. Carefully clip the seam allowances at the intersection of the squares; clip up to, but not through, the stitching. Press the seam allowances in a clockwise direction. Make 50 four-patch units.

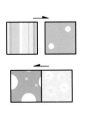

Make 50.

5 Sew 13 four-patch units together end to end. Make two for the side borders. Sew 12 four-patch units together end to end. Make two for the top and bottom borders. Press the seam allowances in either direction. Sew the side borders to the quilt top first, and then add the top and bottom borders.

Finishing the Quilt

Go to ShopMartingale.com/HowtoQuilt if you need more information on finishing techniques.

1 Layer and baste your quilt, and quilt as desired.

2 Using the remaining blue floral 2½"-wide strips, prepare and attach the binding.

Quilt assembly

Rocky Road

When fabrics remind you of your all-time favorite ice cream flavor, how can you resist? Designer Kathy Brown felt no guilt about indulging her love of rocky road with an assortment of nutty, chocolaty, marshmallowy colors. And what a decadent, delightful concoction it turned out to be!

FINISHED QUILT: 40½" × 56½" • **FINISHED BLOCK:** 4" × 4"

Designed by Kathy Brown; pieced by Linda Reed; quilted by Carol Hilton

Materials

Yardage is based on 42"-wide fabric.

24 precut strips, 2½" × 42", of assorted cream tone on tones for blocks

15 precut strips, 2½" × 42", of assorted dark brown prints for blocks and binding

15 precut strips, 2½" × 42", of assorted medium brown prints for blocks and binding

3 yards of fabric for backing

47" × 63" piece of batting

Making the Blocks

Press the seam allowances as indicated by the arrows, or as otherwise instructed.

1. With right sides together, sew a cream strip to each of 12 assorted dark brown strips to make 12 strip sets. Repeat to sew a cream strip to each of 12 assorted medium brown strips to make 12 strip sets. Set aside the remaining dark brown and medium brown strips for the binding.

Make 12.

Make 12.

2. Referring to "Cutting Triangles" on page 9, cut six 90° double-strip triangles from each strip set.

3. Lay a 90° triangle face up on your cutting mat. Place a 6" square ruler on the triangle, lining up the bottom edge of the ruler with the bottom raw edge of the triangle, and the right edge of the 6" ruler with the top of the triangle.

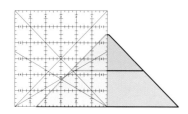

4. Using a rotary cutter, cut the triangle in half along the edge of the 6" ruler, creating two mirror-image triangles. Repeat with the remaining 90° triangles and arrange eight sets of 36 triangles each:
   - cream tip/dark brown strip pointing left
   - cream tip/dark brown strip pointing right
   - dark brown tip/cream strip pointing left
   - dark brown tip/cream strip pointing right
   - cream tip/medium brown strip pointing left
   - cream tip/medium brown strip pointing right
   - medium brown tip/cream strip pointing left
   - medium brown tip/cream strip pointing right

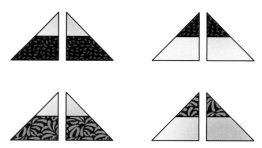

Make 36 of each.

5. With right sides together, sew a cream tip/dark brown strip pointing right triangle to a cream tip/dark brown strip pointing left triangle as shown; press. Repeat to make a total of 36 blocks. Sew the remaining triangles together in the same manner to make the number of blocks indicated of each color combination. (You'll have a total of eight triangles left over.) Kathy recommends starching each block to preserve the bias edges of the triangles.

Make 36.

Make 35.   Make 34.   Make 35.

Assembling the Quilt Top

1 Lay out 14 rows of 10 blocks each as shown.

2 Sew the blocks together into rows, and then sew the rows together.

Finishing the Quilt

Go to ShopMartingale.com/HowtoQuilt if you need more information on finishing techniques.

1 Layer and baste your quilt, and quilt as desired.

2 Using the remaining brown 2½"-wide strips, prepare and attach the binding.

Quilt assembly

String Square

This String Square design is a great choice when you need a quilt in a hurry. With strip piecing you can whip up the blocks in no time, and the wide borders let you finish quickly. Use one of your favorite prints for the border and choose the other fabrics to coordinate with it.

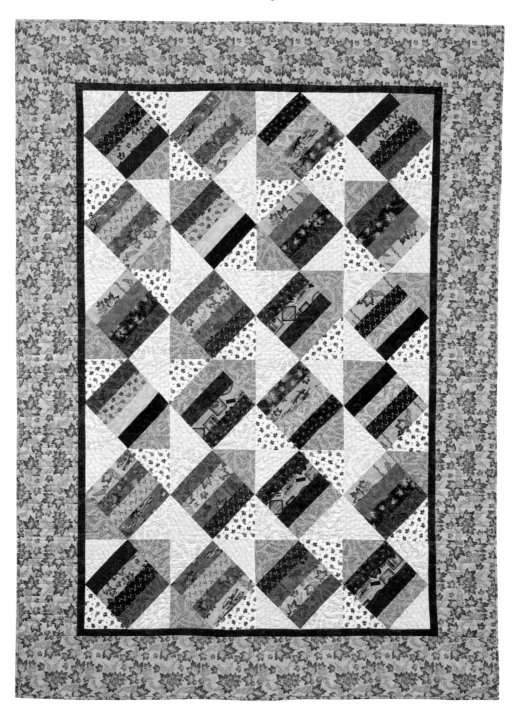

FINISHED QUILT: 63¼" × 85⅞" • **FINISHED BLOCK:** 8" × 8"

Designed by Nancy J. Martin; pieced by Cleo Nollette; quilted by Shelly Nolte

Materials

Yardage is based on 42"-wide fabric.

48 strips, 2½" × 22", of assorted prints for blocks

½ yard *each* of 4 light prints for alternate blocks and setting triangles

⅜ yard of dark print for inner border

2⅓ yards of large-scale floral for outer border and bias binding

5¼ yards of fabric for backing

72" × 94" piece of batting

Cutting

From *each* of the 4 light prints, cut:*

4 squares, 9¼" × 9¼" (16 total); cut the squares into quarters diagonally to yield 64 triangles (4 are extra)

5 squares, 6⅝" × 6⅝" (20 total); cut the squares in half diagonally to yield 40 triangles (4 are extra)

From the dark print, cut:

6 strips, 1½" × 42"

From the large-scale floral, cut:

7 strips, 8¼" × 42"

309" of 2¼"-wide bias strips

Be sure to keep the triangles cut from different-sized squares separate so that you will have the straight grain along the outer edges of the quilt. Label them if desired.

Making the Blocks

Press the seam allowances as indicated by the arrows, or as otherwise instructed.

1 Sew the 2½" × 22" strips into random sets of four strips each. Make 12 strip sets. Cut each set into 2 segments, 8½" wide, to make a total of 24 segments.

8½"

Make 12 strip sets.
Cut 24 segments.

2 Make 15 alternate blocks by stitching together four triangles cut from the 9¼" squares, using one of each light print.

Make 15.

3 Make 16 half blocks for the quilt edges by stitching together two triangles cut from the 6⅝" squares, using different light prints. Reserve four triangles for the quilt corners.

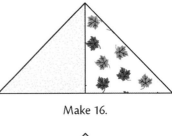

Make 16.

Reserve 4 for corners.

Assembling the Quilt Top

1 Arrange the blocks cut from strip sets (oriented in the same direction), alternate blocks, and half blocks in diagonal rows.

2 Sew the blocks together into rows; press. Sew the rows together and press, adding the corner triangles last.

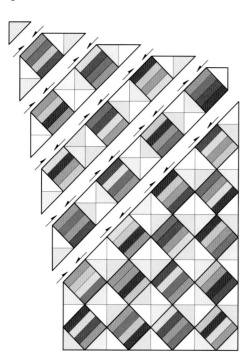

3 Join the dark print 1½"-wide strips end to end. Measure the length of the quilt top through the center. Cut two strips to that measurement and sew them to the sides of the quilt top. Press the seam allowances away from the center. Measure the width of the quilt top through the center, including the borders just added. Cut two strips to that measurement and sew them to the top and bottom of the quilt top to complete the inner border. Press the seam allowances away from the center.

4 Repeat with the floral 8¼"-wide strips to add the outer border.

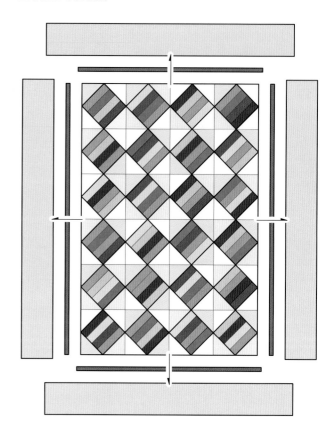

Finishing the Quilt

Go to ShopMartingale.com/HowtoQuilt if you need more information on finishing techniques.

1 Layer and baste your quilt, and quilt as desired.

2 Using the floral 2¼"-wide bias strips, prepare and attach the binding.

Fireworks

////////////

A red-white-and-blue quilt is a can't-miss accessory—as a blanket for summer picnics, a tablecloth for a Fourth of July gathering, or a star-spangled show of spirit any time of year.

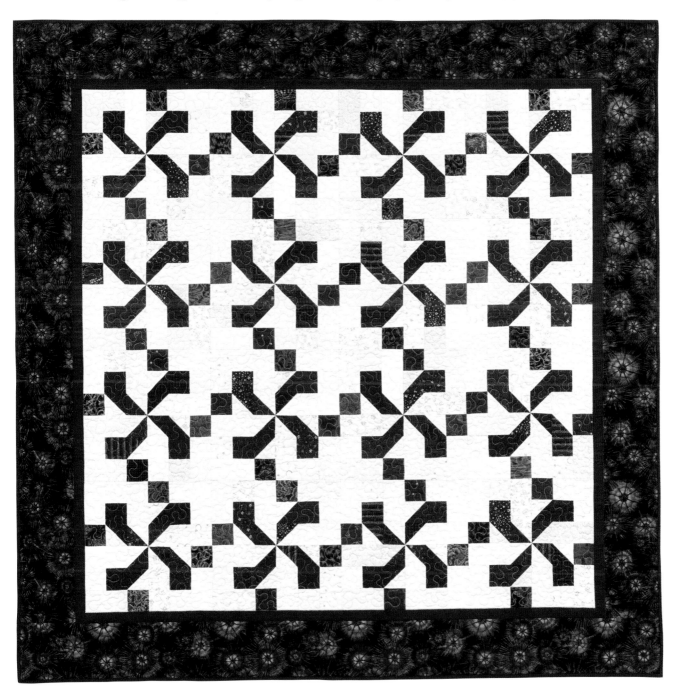

FINISHED QUILT: 61½" × 61½" • **FINISHED BLOCK:** 12" × 12"

Designed, pieced, and quilted by Kim Brackett

Materials

Yardage is based on 42"-wide fabric.

28 precut strips, 2½" × 42", of assorted white prints for blocks

13 precut strips, 2½" × 42", of assorted red prints for blocks

½ yard *total* of assorted blue print scraps for blocks

⅞ yard of dark red print for inner border and binding

1⅛ yards of dark blue print for outer border

4¼ yards of fabric for backing

68" × 68" piece of batting

Cutting

From *each* of 10 white print strips, cut:

3 rectangles, 2½" × 6½" (30 total)*
2 rectangles, 2½" × 4½" (20 total)**
4 squares, 2½" × 2½" (40 total)***

From *each* of 9 white print strips, cut:

2 rectangles, 2½" × 6½" (18 total)*
3 rectangles, 2½" × 4½" (27 total)**
4 squares, 2½" × 2½" (36 total)***

From *each* of 9 white print strips, cut:

2 rectangles, 2½" × 6½" (18 total)*
2 rectangles, 2½" × 4½" (18 total)**
6 squares, 2½" × 2½" (54 total)***

From *each* of the 13 red print strips, cut:

5 rectangles, 2½" × 4½" (65 total; 1 is extra)
5 squares, 2½" × 2½" (65 total; 1 is extra)

From the blue print scraps, cut:

2½"-wide strips; crosscut into 64 squares, 2½" × 2½"

From the dark red print, cut:

6 strips, 1½" × 42"
7 strips, 2½" × 42"

From the dark blue print, cut:

6 strips, 6" × 42"

There will be a total of 66 white print 2½" × 6½" rectangles; 2 will be extra.

**There will be a total of 65 white print 2½" × 4½" rectangles; 1 will be extra.*

***There will be a total of 130 white print 2½" squares; 2 will be extra.*

Time to whittle down your fabric stash? To cut your blocks from scraps rather than using precut 2½" strips as listed in "Materials" at left, follow these instructions.

From white print scraps, cut:

64 rectangles, 2½" × 6½"
64 rectangles, 2½" × 4½"
128 squares, 2½" × 2½"

From red print scraps, cut:

64 rectangles, 2½" × 4½"
64 squares, 2½" × 2½"

From blue print scraps, cut:

64 squares, 2½" × 2½"

Making the Blocks

Press the seam allowances as indicated by the arrows, or as otherwise instructed.

1. Draw a diagonal line from corner to corner on the wrong side of a red 2½" square. Place the marked square on one end of a white 2½" × 6½" rectangle, right sides together and corners aligned. Sew on the line. Trim the excess corner fabric, leaving a ¼" seam allowance, and press. Make four for each of the 16 blocks.

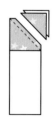 

Make 4
for each block.

2 Repeat step 1 using a white 2½" square and a red 2½" × 4½" rectangle. Make four for each of the 16 blocks.

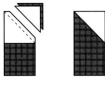

Make 4
for each block.

3 Sew a white 2½" square to the bottom of the unit from step 2. Make four for each of the 16 blocks.

Make 4
for each block.

4 Sew a blue 2½" square to a white 2½" × 4½" rectangle. Make four for each of the 16 blocks.

Make 4
for each block.

5 Sew together the units from steps 1, 3, and 4 as shown. Make four units for each of the 16 blocks.

Make 4
for each block.

6 Join four of the units from step 5 as shown to complete one block. Carefully clip the seam allowances at the intersection of the units; clip up to, but not through, the stitching. Press the seam allowances in a counterclockwise direction. Make 16 blocks.

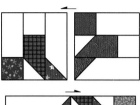

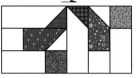

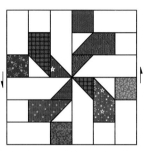

Make 16.

Assembling the Quilt Top

1 Lay out four rows of four blocks each.

2 Sew the blocks together into rows; press. Sew the rows together and press the seam allowances in one direction.

3 Join the dark red 1½"-wide strips end to end. Measure the length of the quilt top through the center. Cut two strips to that measurement and sew them to the sides of the quilt top. Press the seam allowances away from the center. Measure the width of the quilt top through the center, including the borders just added. Cut two strips to that measurement and sew them to the top and bottom of the quilt top to complete the inner border. Press the seam allowances away from the center.

4 Repeat with the blue 6"-wide strips to add the outer border.

Finishing the Quilt

Go to ShopMartingale.com/HowtoQuilt if you need more information on finishing techniques.

1 Layer and baste your quilt, and quilt as desired.

2 Using the dark red 2½"-wide strips, prepare and attach the binding.

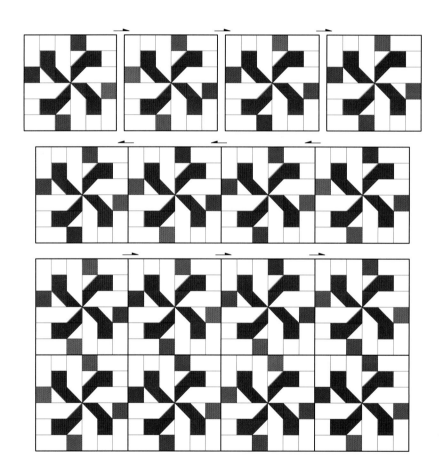

The Big Book of Strip Quilts

Split the Difference

Rich florals radiate with a prismatic quality in a complex-looking design, but the construction process is quite manageable thanks to squares and rectangles easily cut from strips.

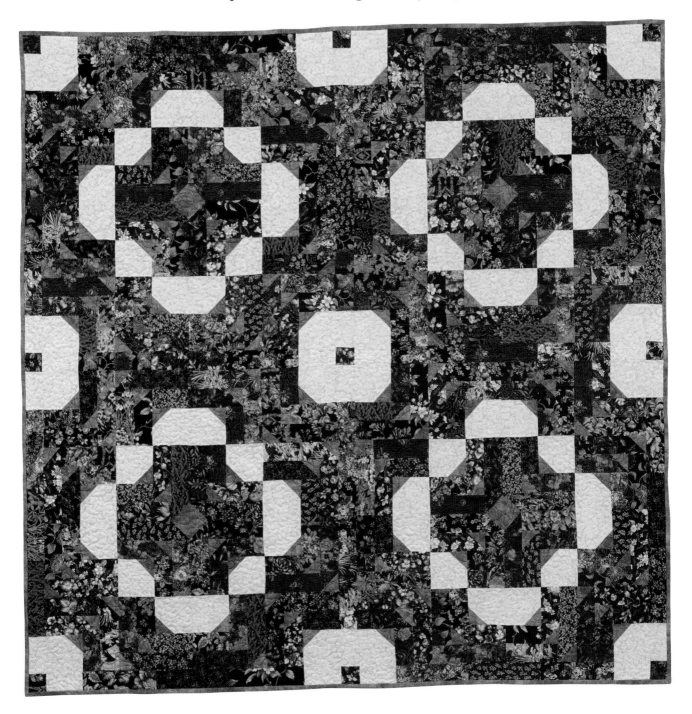

FINISHED QUILT: 70½" × 70½" • **FINISHED BLOCK:** 8" × 8"

Designed, pieced, and quilted by Cathy Wierzbicki

Materials

Yardage is based on 42"-wide fabric.

54 precut strips, 2½" × 42", of assorted dark florals for blocks and sashing

12 precut strips, 2½" × 42", of accent fabric for blocks

1⅜ yards of light print for blocks and sashing

⅔ yard of fabric for binding

4¼ yards of fabric for backing

77" × 77" piece of batting

Cutting

From the 54 dark floral strips, cut a *total* of:

100 rectangles, 2½" × 8½" (D)

128 rectangles, 2½" × 6½" (C)

64 rectangles, 2½" × 4½" (B)

9 squares, 2½" × 2½" (G)

From the light print, cut:

10 strips, 4½" × 42"; crosscut into:

    64 squares, 4½" × 4½" (A)

    24 rectangles, 2½" × 4½" (F)

From the 12 accent-fabric strips, cut a *total* of:

192 squares, 2½" × 2½" (E)

From the binding fabric, cut:

8 strips, 2½" × 42"

Making the Blocks

Press the seam allowances as indicated by the arrows, or as otherwise instructed.

1. Draw a diagonal line from corner to corner on the wrong side of an E square. Place the marked square on one corner of an A square, right sides together and corners aligned. Sew on the line. Trim the excess corner fabric, leaving a ¼" seam allowance, and press. Make 64.

Make 64.

2. Referring to the technique used in step 1, place a marked E square on one end of a C rectangle. Stitch, trim, and press. Make 64 units with C rectangles and 64 units with D rectangles, being careful to position the seams as shown.

Make 64 of each.

3. Sew a B rectangle to the top edge of each unit from step 1 as shown. Sew one E/C unit from step 2 to the left side. Make 64.

  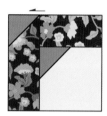

Make 64.

4. Sew a C rectangle to the top edge of each unit from step 3 as shown. Sew one E/D unit from step 2 to the left side. Make 64.

 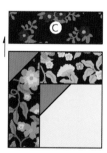

Make 64.

5 Arrange 16 blocks from step 4 in four rows of four blocks each, rotating them as shown. Sew the blocks together into rows, and then sew the rows together. Make four.

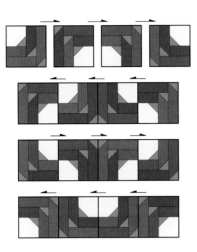

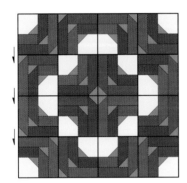

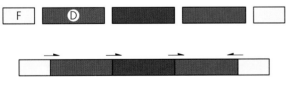

Make 4.

Assembling the Quilt Top

1 Arrange and sew two F rectangles and three D rectangles together as shown to make a sashing unit. Make 12.

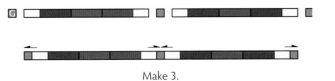

Make 12.

2 Arrange and sew three G squares and two sashing units from step 1 together as shown. Make three.

Make 3.

3 Arrange and sew three sashing units from step 1 and two blocks together as shown. Make two.

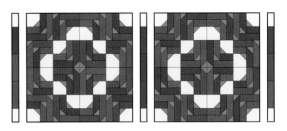

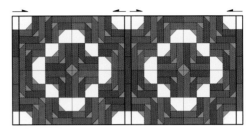

Make 2.

4 Arrange the block and sashing rows from steps 2 and 3, alternating them as shown. Sew the rows together and press.

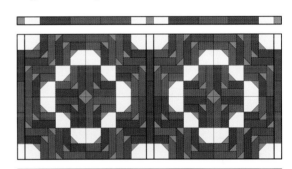

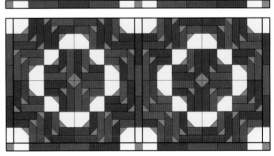

Assembly diagram

Finishing the Quilt

Go to ShopMartingale.com/HowtoQuilt if you need more information on finishing techniques.

1 Layer and baste your quilt, and quilt as desired.

2 Using the 2½"-wide binding strips, prepare and attach the binding.

Split the Difference Table Topper

Featuring a different layout but the same block design as its namesake quilt on page 215, this topper is half the size but just as mesmerizing.

FINISHED QUILT: 32½" × 32½" • **FINISHED BLOCK:** 8" × 8"

Designed, pieced, and quilted by Cathy Wierzbicki

Materials

Yardage is based on 42"-wide fabric.

12 precut strips, 2½" × 42", of assorted dark florals for blocks

3 precut strips, 2½" × 42", of accent fabric for blocks

⅓ yard of light print for blocks

⅜ yard of fabric for binding

1⅛ yards of fabric for backing

37" × 37" piece of batting

Cutting

From the 12 dark floral strips, cut a *total* of:

16 rectangles, 2½" × 8½" (D)

32 rectangles, 2½" × 6½" (C)

16 rectangles, 2½" × 4½" (B)

From the light print, cut:

2 strips, 4½" × 42"; crosscut into 16 squares, 4½" × 4½" (A)

From the 3 accent-fabric strips, cut a *total* of:

48 squares, 2½" × 2½" (E)

From the binding fabric, cut:

4 strips, 2½" × 42"

Making the Table Topper

1 Refer to "Making the Blocks," steps 1–4, on page 216 of the Split the Difference quilt to make 16 blocks as shown.

Make 16.

2 Arrange and sew four blocks from step 1 in two rows of two blocks each as shown. Sew the rows together. Make four.

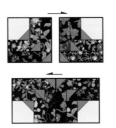
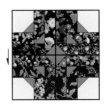

Make 4.

3 Arrange and sew the blocks from step 2 in two rows of two blocks each as shown. Sew the rows together.

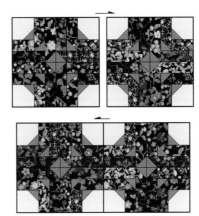

Finishing the Table Topper

Go to ShopMartingale.com/HowtoQuilt if you need more information on finishing techniques.

1 Layer and baste your table topper, and quilt as desired.

2 Using the 2½"-wide binding strips, prepare and attach the binding.

Around the Block

A big achievement deserves a stunning gift. Whether commemorating a graduation, retirement, or some other special event in between, express your accolades with a design that is simple yet effective, bold yet instantly classic.

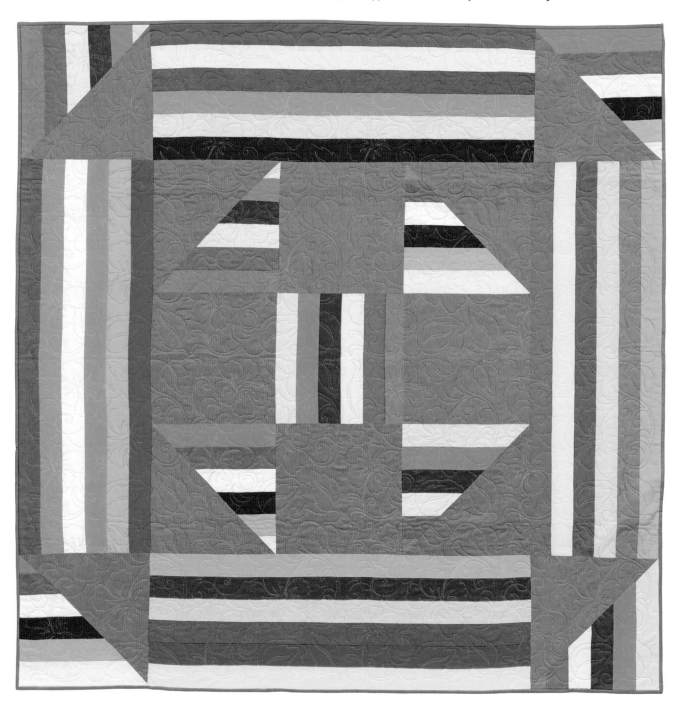

FINISHED QUILT: 60½" × 60½" • **FINISHED CENTER BLOCK:** 36" × 36"

Designed by Rachel Griffith; pieced by Molly Culley; quilted by Darla Padilla

Materials

Yardage is based on 42"-wide fabric.

36 precut strips, 2½" × 42", of assorted solids for
    center block and border
1¼ yards of gray solid for center block and border
⅝ yard of fabric for binding
3¾ yards of fabric for backing
67" × 67" piece of batting

Cutting

From the gray solid, cut:

3 strips, 12½" × 42"; crosscut into:
    4 squares, 12½" × 12½"
    4 rectangles, 12½" × 13¼"

From the binding fabric, cut:

7 strips, 2¼" × 42"

Making the Strip Blocks

Press the seam allowances as indicated by the arrows,
or as otherwise instructed.

1 Join six assorted solid 2½" × 42" strips to make a
strip set. Repeat to make a total of six strip sets.
They should measure 12½" tall.

Make 6 strip sets.

2 From one strip set, cut one 12½" square and
two 12½" × 13¼" rectangles. From another
strip set, cut two 12½" × 13¼" rectangles. From
the remaining strip sets, cut a total of four
12½" × 36½" rectangles.

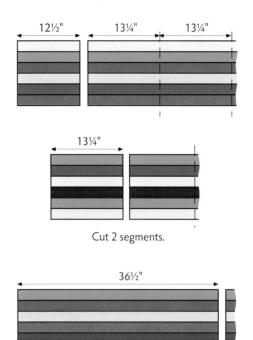

Cut 2 segments.

Cut 4 segments.

Making the Pieced Squares

1 On the wrong side of each gray 12½" × 13¼"
rectangle, make a mark along the edge of the
fabric, ⅜" from the bottom-left corner as shown.
Make a second mark ⅛" from the top-right
corner. Draw a diagonal line connecting the
marks. Place the marked rectangle right sides
together with a 12½" × 13¼" strip-set segment,
making sure the segment is oriented as shown.
Sew ¼" from each side of the marked line.

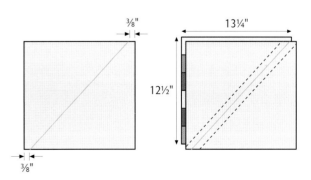

2 Cut the rectangles apart on the marked line and press. The squares should measure 12½" × 12½".

Make 2.

3 Repeat steps 1 and 2 using the remaining gray rectangles and 12½" × 13¼" strip-set segments, making sure to orient the segments as shown. Make six of these pieced squares.

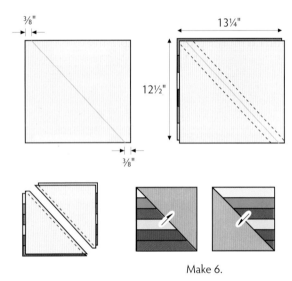

Make 6.

Assembling the Quilt Top

1 Lay out four pieced squares, the 12½" strip-set square, and the gray 12½" squares in three rows, orienting the pieced squares as shown below.

2 Sew the squares together into rows, press, and then sew the rows together.

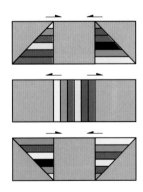 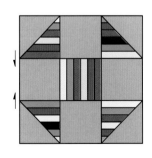

3 Sew 12½" × 36½" strip-set rectangles to opposite sides of the center block. Sew pieced squares to the ends of the two remaining strip-set rectangles. Sew these strips to the top and bottom of the quilt top.

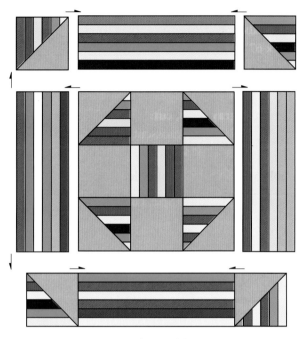

Quilt assembly

Finishing the Quilt

Go to ShopMartingale.com/HowtoQuilt if you need more information on finishing techniques.

1 Layer and baste your quilt, and quilt as desired.

2 Using the 2¼"-wide binding strips, prepare and attach the binding.

All about Precut Strips

Different fabric companies call precut strips by different names, such as Jelly Rolls or Bali Pops. Each strip in the bundle measures 2½" wide and was cut across the width of the fabric (42"). Many bundles include 40 strips, but that too can vary.

Fabric companies started making precut bundles to promote their fabric lines, and one bundle usually contains fabrics from one line, resulting in a group of fabrics with similar colors and patterns. Depending on the number of fabrics in the line there may be duplicate strips in the bundle.

Using precut strips can make quick work of piecing a quilt top, but you don't have to purchase precuts to make any of the quilts in this book. If you prefer, you can cut 2½" × 42" strips from yardage.

If you're new to using precut strips, there are a few things that will be helpful for you to know.

Unwrapping Precut Strips

To keep your long strips from tangling, gently ease the bundle open and clip or secure the strips at one end. Pin the ends of the strips to your ironing board to hold them in place, and then fan them apart and choose the strips you want by easing them away from the rest.

Don't Prewash!

If you prefer to prewash your fabrics before cutting and sewing, learn to resist the temptation to wash or even rinse your precut fabric strips. Washing could cause the fabric to fray, ravel, or shrink, resulting in pieces that are no longer an accurate size.

You can test a strip for bleeding by spritzing it with a little water and pressing with steam between two pieces of muslin, being careful not to stretch the strip out of shape. Examine the muslin for any running or bleeding of color. If you're worried about

fabrics bleeding when it comes time to wash your finished quilt, use this trick from Carrie Nelson of Miss Rosie's Quilt Company: Toss a Shout Color Catcher sheet in the washing machine. These sheets resemble fabric-softener dryer sheets, but they're made to catch any dyes that may run out of fabric during the wash cycle and prevent them from bleeding onto other parts of your quilt.

Working with Pinked Edges

Don't trim the pinked edges off any of the precut fabrics; you won't have enough fabric to make the quilt if you do. When aligning your fabrics for crosscutting or sewing, use the outer points of the pinked edges as the edge of the fabrics so that your ¼" seam allowances will be accurate.

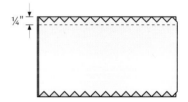

Use It Up

If your project ends up looking a bit on the scrappy side, consider making the binding scrappy, too. Precut 2½"-wide strips are just the right width for making double-fold binding. So to use up leftover strips (full-length or partial strips), consider stitching them together end to end, using a diagonal seam, to give your quilt the perfect scrappy ending. Just be sure all of the ends of the strips are trimmed with the angles facing in the same direction.

Leftover strips can also be used to make a pieced back for your quilt. Simply sew the strips together along their long edges to create a striped panel.

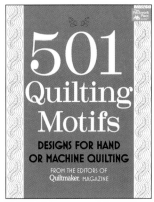

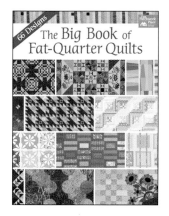
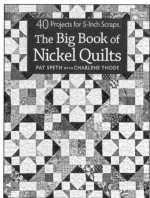

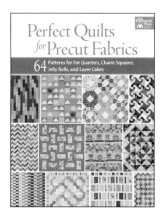

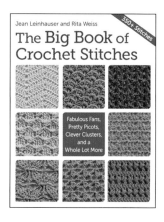